STRONGER

FROM TRIALS
TO TRIATHLETE
TO TRIUMPHANT

Lindsey Jacobs

STONEBROOK
PUBLISHING

Stonebrook Publishing
Saint Louis, Missouri

A STONEBROOK PUBLISHING BOOK

©2020 by Lindsey Jacobs

This book was guided in development and
edited by Nancy L. Erickson, The Book Professor®
TheBookProfessor.com

Library of Congress Control Number: 2019915913

ISBN: 978-1-7339958-4-9

www.stonebrookpublishing.net

PRINTED IN THE UNITED STATES OF AMERICA

10 9 8 7 6 5 4 3 2 1

STRONGER

Lindsey Jacobs

For Dad

It is well, it is well with my soul.

CONTENTS

1: Trapped **1**

2: Laying the Foundation **9**

3: The Making of an Athlete **15**

4: Rebirth of a Runner **21**

5: Too Many Losses **31**

6: Bottoming Out **43**

7: Glimpsing Hope **53**

8: Breaking Up **61**

9: Making Up **67**

10: Finding Courage **73**

11: Taking Big Steps **77**

12: Facing the Truth **83**

13: Testing the Waters **89**

14: Learning New Skills **99**

15: Valuable Lessons **105**

16: Putting It All Together **115**

17: Ditching Excuses **123**

18: Taking Chances **131**

19: Timing Is Everything **137**

20: It Takes a Village **141**

21: On My Way **153**

22: IRONMAN Arizona 2014 **155**

23: Laying It All on the Line **163**

24: Finishing Strong **175**

Rambling Runner Girl's Timeline
of Significant Races **185**

Acknowledgments **187**

Book Club Discussion Questions **191**

About the Author **193**

1: TRAPPED

I shot up in bed as if all the air had been sucked out of the room. My heart pounded in my ears, and I gasped loudly. Even as my sleepy eyes tried to adjust, I could see the shadowy figure looming in the middle of the room.

"Wha . . . who's there?" I asked the darkness.

"It's just me." He sounded annoyed. "Why are you so freaked out? What's wrong with you?"

My husband had been working in Chicago and wasn't due back until the following afternoon, so it caught me completely off guard to see him standing in our bedroom in the middle of the night.

I pulled my knees up to my chest, wrapped my arms around them, and tried to catch my breath.

"What are you doing here? You didn't tell me you were coming back early." I glanced at the clock. It read 2:28 a.m.

"You never asked," he said accusingly.

That was true. I hadn't been in the habit of calling to check in with him on a regular basis. He typically tried to touch base with the kids when he traveled. But we'd been through so much unresolved counseling and had talked things to death. So I didn't feel as if I had all that much left to say to him. He was often angry at the end of phone calls when I didn't say, "I love you." I'd long since lost those feelings and could no longer form the words just to appease him.

"You never asked."

His words hung in the air. My mind drifted back to other times he'd said them. Apparently, it was my fault he didn't feel the need to inform me of his oddly timed arrival in the middle of my REM sleep. But I'd become accustomed to the fact that everything was my fault. It was part of the reason I wanted to escape.

He disappeared into the bathroom. I took the opportunity to change out of my sweat-soaked T-shirt.

As he walked back into the bedroom, he noticed the change. "What are you doing? Why did you change clothes?"

"I didn't feel like wearing tha—" I started.

"Is someone else here?" he demanded.

"What? No, of course not!"

"Why are you acting so weird?"

"You mean other than the fact that you showed up unannounced in the middle of the night and scared the crap out of me?" I shot back. It wasn't the first time I'd felt as if I was being spied on, and it wouldn't be the last.

"It's my house!" he declared. "I can show up whenever I want!"

"Okay, but I'm just saying, it would've been nice if you'd given me a heads-up since it's so late," I argued.

"And I'm just saying, it'd be nice if you showed a little more interest in my being here," he spat. "I still think you're acting weird. What's really going on?"

I was certain he'd discovered my plan to meet with a divorce attorney in the morning and had come home early to try to stop me. But I wasn't about to tip my hand.

"Nothing!" I raised my voice as I grabbed my phone off the nightstand and headed for the door. He stepped in front of me to block my path. "Where do you think you're going?"

"I need some space. Give me a minute," I answered, steering to the right and stepping into my enormous walk-in closet. His erratic behavior was making me uncomfortable, and I wanted to call my mom for reassurance.

"Why are you taking your phone?" he demanded.

"I was . . . I wanted . . ." I struggled to find words. "I want to call my mom," I said finally, trying to close the closet door.

"Give me your phone!" he ordered, blocking the door with his foot. I pushed, but he wouldn't budge. He forced the door open and tried to grab the phone from my hand. I dodged to get around him, but his frame blocked the doorway. He had me backed into a corner with nowhere to go. Should I call the police instead? But in all the times his rage had frightened me, he'd never hit or physically threatened me. What would I tell the police? That my husband was angry because I changed my T-shirt? They'd just laugh at me.

"Let me out!" I shouted, my entire body shaking.

He refused to move. I tried to push him out of the way. Despite his lanky body, he far outweighed me in pounds and strength.

"You're physically assaulting me," he mocked accusingly. I was concerned he could use that against me, so I took my hands off him, defeated. Never mind the fact that he was using brute intimidation to corner me in a closet. My head was spinning.

I was trapped, physically trapped in a closet. But it was so much more than that. For years, I'd been trapped in a cell without bars, a room with no walls or doors, a box with no lid. I was paralyzed, unable to move. I needed to break free. I needed to escape the invisible jail that locked me inside myself. But how? I was terrified. Even if I managed to get away, he'd always make freedom an impossibility.

In that closet, all the red flags I'd tried to ignore—the angry outbursts, the belittling, the intimidation, the humiliation and invalidation—swarmed me. I was drowning in little red flags.

The sound of the bedroom door opening cut through the screaming in my head. I heard a small voice ask, "Dad, what are you doing here?"

Our six-year-old son, Ethan, who, I'd always joked, had the Jacobs gene for being able to sleep through everything, had heard our scuffle and come down the hall to see what was going on.

In a gentler tone, his father repeated what he'd told me a few minutes earlier: his plans had changed, and he'd decided to drive back late rather than wait until morning.

"Why didn't you tell us you were coming home?" Ethan's little boy voice creaked.

"Well, you were already asleep when I made the decision."

"Why are you guys fighting?" Ethan asked, rubbing his eyes.

"Your dad scared me because I wasn't expecting him," I interjected, making excuses for my husband's behavior, as usual. "Come on, buddy, let's get you back to bed."

I was still shaking as I tried to even out my breathing so my son wouldn't read my emotions.

We walked down the hall, and I tucked Ethan back into bed, grateful he had defused a volatile situation. I handed him the blue blanket he affectionately called Baba and kissed him on the forehead. Taking a deep breath, I made my way back down the hall, dreading the fire I knew I had to face.

My husband had already claimed his spot in the bed in a silent act of defiance. He knew how uncomfortable I was sharing a bed while our marriage was in such turmoil.

Almost as soon as I closed the bedroom door, it swung open again. Ethan, dragging his Baba behind him, refused to sleep in his own room. I let him climb into the middle of the king-size bed as I turned out the light.

I appreciated the barrier between me and his dad. Ethan's sweet presence grounded me and gave me comfort. He quietly reached over in the dark and folded his tiny hand into mine. His dad's breathing quickly gave way to the sound of sleep, but I couldn't do more than fitfully doze for the next few hours until the sunlight began creeping in. I wasn't convinced Ethan had slept either. We lay next to each other in silence until I roused him to get ready for school.

I didn't know how to find the strength or the courage to break free, but I knew I had to try. It was a matter of showing my children that you can only stand down for so long, that there comes a point when you have to stand up, be strong, and take your power back. It was a matter of survival. I needed to escape. It was time.

Crisis on the Horizon

Our relationship hadn't always been like that. There'd been a subtle shift over time. In the beginning, it had felt as if we were destined to be together.

In the spring of 1998, my final semester at Michigan State University, my schedule was very light. To maintain eligibility on the varsity women's rowing team, I had to register only for the classes required to complete my degree. That meant I had one class.

I joined my team for daily practices and went to strength and conditioning three mornings a week. On Tuesday evenings, my three-hour class met immediately after practice. Racing filled most of my weekends. My life consisted primarily of rowing and looking for a job.

My area of study was family community services. I'd always known I wanted to work with children. In one of my child ecology courses, I'd read *There Are No Children Here*, a book about two young boys who grew up in the Henry Horner Homes, a housing project on the west side of Chicago. I'd long planned to move to Chicago after graduation, but the true story of those boys fueled that fire and strengthened my desire to work with inner-city youth.

That spring, I made the four-hour drive between East Lansing and Chicago multiple times for interviews and apartment hunting. Sometimes I managed to slip in an occasional Cubs game. Another reason I wanted to move to Chicago was that, being a Jacobs, I was born a sixth-generation Cubs fan.

One unseasonably warm Sunday in April, I had a rare day off from practice and racing. So along with the guy I'd been dating off and on for the last two years, I drove into the city for my first game of the season in the bleachers at Wrigley Field.

We bought our tickets and hiked up the ramp to find seats somewhere in the stands overlooking left-center field. Spotting an opening, we nabbed two seats.

As the game began, it became apparent that we'd landed in the middle of a fairly large group. A new attorney who'd recently been sworn in to the Missouri Bar Association was celebrating with several friends and members of his extended family. We became part of their group as the smaller cousins were passed among us, one of whom would, a couple years later, be my flower girl. At one point, I stood to take off my sweatshirt, accidentally spilling my beer on the woman who would one day become my mother-in-law.

The game, as well as the company we kept that day, was entertaining. We cheered the Cubbies on to victory and shared camaraderie and plenty of laughter.

As the day ended and we prepared to drive back, my then-boyfriend said to the tall new attorney, "Hey, my girlfriend is moving to Chicago in a couple of months. Can I get your number so she can call you if she needs anything? She doesn't know anyone here."

The attorney obligingly wrote his number on the game ticket, and I tucked it into the back pocket of my cutoff jean shorts. That ticket lay on my desk back in East Lansing until I packed everything into boxes and loaded them up for my big move to the city. I'd landed a job as a crisis counselor with Youth Outreach Services and would start at the beginning of June.

I settled quickly and easily into my new job and tiny studio apartment on the north side of Chicago. I liked the girls I worked with, but none of them lived anywhere near me. I didn't know anyone in my neighborhood, so most weekends I drove home to see my family and friends.

One evening, with nothing to do, I stood holding that ticket in one hand and my cordless phone in the other. It had been months since I'd met the guy. Would he even remember me? I dialed the number.

He answered.

"Yeah, hi. I don't know if you remember me, but this is Lindsey. We met in the bleachers at Wrigley a while back."

He remembered, which surprised me. I'd always had a great memory for people, but I knew not everyone did. More than that, I believed myself to be somewhat forgettable.

After we talked for a bit, he said, "Hey, I have to go. I'm on my way to watch the Bulls game with some friends. You're welcome to meet us if you want."

The Chicago Bulls were making a run in the NBA playoffs, with Michael Jordan leading the way. I wasn't a basketball fan, but I didn't have anything else to do. So I figured, "Why not?"

"Sure," I said.

He told me they'd be at Corner Pocket, a bar in Wrigleyville. When I got there, the place was jammed. The game was more than half over, and I squeezed through the crowd, trying to locate him.

"Hey, you found us!" he said as I arrived at the table. He did a quick round of introductions over the noise. "What's with the backpack?" he asked.

I explained that as a crisis counselor, I had to be prepared in the event of a crisis, and I was on call that night. In a crisis, I might be called to a police station to find temporary placement for a minor who'd either run away from home or been kicked out. To be honest, I felt like a complete dork carting around a backpack of my work supplies, but I showed off my pager, and everyone had a good laugh.

"Are you a doctor or a drug dealer?" someone teased.

I was very insecure, but as my new friend and his friends welcomed and included me, I felt as if I belonged somewhere. He and I had an immediate connection, and it wasn't long before we started spending a fair amount of time together.

It also wasn't long before the long-distance thing, among other issues, became a strain on the two-year relationship I'd begun during college. I'd gotten wind that my boyfriend had cheated on me. Without having the opportunity to talk face-to-face, we broke up in a heated phone call.

"It's over!" I yelled into the cordless receiver before disconnecting.

Despite my anger, I missed having closure to the relationship and started moving on before I was healed.

My Chicago attorney friend began to pursue me—a girl who hid her inner insecurities well. On the outside, however, I appeared to be confident in my uniqueness, and he often commented that I always seemed to be smiling.

He was charming and took me everywhere. We went on late-night bike rides to Navy Pier, enjoyed great dinners, and attended outdoor music festivals where we danced under the stars. We took in Cubs games at the Friendly Confines as often as we could and watched sports history made between Mark

McGuire and Sammy Sosa, as well as the pitching genius of Kerry Wood. Soon we were inseparable.

One humid August night, sitting by the lake, he asked me if I'd be his girlfriend. I hesitated. I knew it was too soon. I wasn't completely over my last boyfriend yet, and we were still getting to know each other.

I mumbled through what I was thinking, but my resistance didn't fly with him. He was pouty, and guilt bubbled inside me. I was afraid if I didn't say yes, he'd give up on me and that would be the end of things. I knew we should wait, but going against what I knew in my heart, I agreed, and we officially became a couple.

Although I was happy, I had concerns about what I'd agreed to. A tiny red flag rose in my gut, but I shoved it aside, the first of many times I ignored my instincts about him.

Two years later, on a grassy knoll just steps from my parents' beach condo overlooking Lake Michigan, we were married on a beautiful July day. The sun was shining, and I was surrounded by people I loved. I looped my arm through my dad's to begin our march down the aisle.

"I feel like a princess," I said to him.

With tears filling his eyes, he responded, "You are a princess, Lindsey." Then he handed his daughter over to another man who promised to take care of her.

We had a lot of good times. I was head over heels in love when I married him. There'd been other red flags that I'd chosen to ignore along the way, but we'd met at Wrigley Field and were married in a town that held so many wonderful childhood memories for me. To anyone on the outside looking in, our life together seemed idyllic. But, of course, things aren't always what they seem.

2: LAYING THE FOUNDATION

"Princess" was certainly not the way I would have described myself growing up. "Tomboy" was a more accurate term. I loved to climb trees, build forts, and trade baseball cards.

One unforgettable day, I realized, quite by accident, that I was born to be a runner. It was Field Day at Kirksville Upper Elementary School. I'd been chosen as the representative for Mrs. Troester's fourth-grade class in the girls' four-hundred-meter run. It was a run, mind you, not a dash, because on short, little nine-year-old legs, one lap around the track is a long haul.

The sun was shining, and the high school bleachers were filled with classmates, teachers, and parents cheering loudly as fourteen of us lined up to toe the start line for the main event of the day. I took a deep breath and tried to shake off the nerves that flooded my body. The butterflies in my stomach caused a wave of nausea.

"On your mark," the announcer bellowed.

We all leaned forward in ready position.

"Get set."

Bang! The gun went off, and our bodies started moving. Arms and legs pumped, and lungs worked to maximum capacity. As we merged toward the inner lane of the track, I was in a less-than-favorable position. When I rounded the first turn, I was, if not dead last, very close to it, but as we came out of the curve into the long straightaway, I began to slingshot past several of the other girls on the track. I edged a little closer to the middle of the pack, but I was still a long way out of first place. Kim Scott, as expected, was leading us all around that huge oval, and there were still a few runners between me and the favored winner.

The sounds of heavy breathing and the crunch of gravel underfoot rang in my ears as we entered the second curve. It was clear that some of the girls were starting to tire and slow down. I was gaining ground, and I could see Kim in front of me. It was time to make my move. Coming into the home stretch toward the finish, there were only two of us. I was in second place by just a few strides. I thought my lungs might explode, but I willed my legs to go faster, and they didn't let me down. We were stride for stride with only a few meters to go. I stepped ahead just as we crossed the line.

I'd won! I'd started out in almost last place, but I'd held on as the underdog and made a come-from-behind win. I was shocked. By the look on Kim's face, she was, too. We'd all thought she had it in the bag. As I turned toward the bleachers, I could see my fourth-grade classmates jumping up and down. My parents waved, and I beamed from ear to ear.

"Lind-sey! Lind-sey! Lind-sey!" they chanted, as I waved back, still trying to catch my breath.

When I arrived home from school later that day, a special surprise was waiting for me on the kitchen table: a congratulations gift in the form of a helium-filled Snoopy balloon. I cherished it. What it represented made it so special. When the chips were down, I didn't give up. I kept pushing and ran my heart out. My parents were proud, my schoolmates were proud, and I was proud of myself.

I'd love to be able to say that from there I went on to become an Olympian, but that wasn't exactly the case. I did begin running with my dad on a regular basis after that. He'd run marathons in my very early years. Whenever I saw him in his running clothes, I'd ask to go out with him. We'd lace up and run a mile or two together.

While we ran, he said things like, "When you run downhill, let the momentum of the hill do the work" and "It's going to get harder when you run uphill. Keep your head up. Keep your eyes forward. It's okay to slow down a little if you have to. Take smaller steps and keep putting one foot in front of the other."

At that time, I thought he was talking only about running. As I got older, I came to realize that my dad was also giving me advice about life in general.

It wasn't long before he decided I was ready to join him at a local 5k race that also included a one-mile kids' run. Andi Schneider, with her red hair blowing out behind her, finished ahead of me that day. But in my cotton shorts and fashion tank top from Walmart, I ran a mile in seven minutes flat. Not too shabby. Andi continued to be my rabbit.

As I hovered on the threshold of adolescence, I ran more 5k races with my dad. It wasn't uncommon in our small town for me to win my age group of fourteen and under because I was usually the only runner in that age group. I earned several medals, and at one race I received a trophy for being the youngest runner to participate.

My friend Angela, who lived just a couple houses down on Shady Lane, had taken up running with us. She became my running partner, so sometimes it was just us two girls. We ran through the neighborhood and out to First Street. We encouraged each other up the big hill to Shepherd Road, where we turned around to go home.

Angela began running 5ks with us, and the day I won that trophy, she lamented being just a few months older than I. The trophy went on display in my room. The little plaque describing it came unglued after a while, but I always displayed it along with all my other medals and running memorabilia.

Cross Country Not for Me

At the end of eighth grade, my parents sat me down one night.

They told me, "We want to let you know, we're moving back to Michigan at the end of the summer."

"What? Why?" I asked, eyes wide and brimming with tears.

They explained that, due to my dad's job change, we'd be moving away from the small town I'd grown to love, back to where I'd been born and lived for most of my younger years. I was devastated.

I hung my head and sat listening. I heard their words, but my heart held on tightly to hope that the plan would change.

The end of the school year was bittersweet. My class was getting ready to start high school, but I wouldn't be joining them. I'd be going to high school at a new place. I still had some friends there from my early years, but it just wasn't the same. I was leaving so much behind.

On my last day at Kirksville Junior High, I said goodbye to many friends I likely wouldn't see much over the summer. I spent the summer doing my usual "summer things," like going to camp, hanging out with my youth group, running with Angela, and spending as much time as possible with my other close friends. I also managed to pack the contents of my room and all my running memorabilia.

In August, the movers came and loaded everything into a huge moving truck. We drove north less than a week before I started my freshman year of high school. We spent a few days at my grandparents' farm on the outskirts of the city. The first day of school, I was up extra early due to the longer-than-normal commute. My dad pulled the minivan up to the curb and dropped me off at a school that seemed utterly immense.

That day was tough. I'd gone from being a contented fish in a reasonably sized pond to being a small fish in a large pond where several schools had merged. My old friends from my elementary days had made new friends and had tight cliques. The people who didn't know me had no clue I was "the new girl," because with three middle schools coming together to form the graduating class of 1993, everyone was new. I felt invisible.

At the end of the day, with a heavy backpack and a heavy heart hidden behind my usual smile, I walked the distance from my new school, past my old neighborhood, past my old elementary school, all the way to my new house. The now-empty truck was parked in the driveway, so my bedroom furniture had been delivered. It was time to set up shop in a new location.

By the second month of school, my algebra teacher, Mr. Brown, who was also the track and cross-country coach, had convinced me to join the team. The abilities I'd been so proud of back in Missouri seemed to pale in comparison to the high school speedsters. I was slow, and running hurt more than it had during my carefree jogs with

Angela. I missed my friends, and I was generally sad. So much had changed, and I wasn't the same girl anymore.

I suffered through that season of cross country, feeling not like a runner or part of the team but like a puzzle piece that didn't fit. I competed in only a handful of races, and running wasn't fun anymore. It had become a chore. I questioned if the sport was really for me.

At the end of the season, I hung up my running shoes, and that was the end of my cross-country career. Mr. Brown spent the next three years exasperating himself trying to teach me algebra while simultaneously trying to convince me to give up cheerleading and return to running. Always a stubborn girl, I stuck to my guns. Running was on hold.

Doing the Right Thing

Eventually, I made some friends that year. In my PE class, I had one friend who didn't stick around after she decided I was too prudish and boring. However, she stayed in my life long enough to convince me to try out for the softball team. Despite my family's deep love of the Chicago Cubs, I'd never actually thrown a baseball. I didn't even own a glove. The night before tryouts, my dad and I drove off to find one.

We lived in mid-Michigan, so naturally we went to Meijer. Meijer is like a combination of Target, Walmart, Kroger, and Toys R Us. They have absolutely everything you could ever want or need, and they're open twenty-four hours a day. I have lots of great memories of driving to Meijer at any time of day or night with my dad to buy a ridiculous assortment of things like batteries, strawberries, and a fishing pole or other random items.

"I'm going to Meijer," Dad would say at 11 o'clock in the evening. "I need socks."

"I'm coming, too!" I'd exclaim, jumping up from whatever I was doing to join him in the car.

But the night before freshman softball tryouts, I needed a glove. We stood in the aisle that displayed athletic gear. He inspected a few gloves and put each one back in turn.

"You don't know what position you'll be playing, so we don't want to get you anything too specific," he said as I watched, not knowing what he meant by that.

I shrugged. "Okay, whatever you think."

"Here. Try this one." He handed me a glove, and I put it on.

"It fits," I said.

"Like a glove," we said in unison and laughed.

I still have that softball glove. It's the only one I've ever used, and it's perfectly broken in. Even though my softball abilities were never that great, I played softball all four years of high school. Our team wasn't especially talented and neither was our coach, but I learned some valuable life lessons about discipline, dedication, and working my butt off.

My best friend, Nikki, a pitcher, had moved to East Lansing at the start of our sophomore year. She needed to throw during the off season, and we were always together anyway, so we spent a lot of time practicing. That led me to pursue the position of catcher.

One cold January day during our senior year, we stayed after school to practice in the gym. Our coach walked over and said to me, "I like your dedication. This is earning you a spot in the starting line-up." He'd made promises before, so I was hesitant, but I let hope fill me anyway.

When opening day of the season came, I found myself sitting on the bench while the snow fell softly around me. My heart and my hopes were shattered.

At the end of the game, I climbed into the front seat of my dad's van. Angry tears spilled from my eyes as I felt my dad's compassionate gaze fall on me.

"I know you're frustrated," he said, "but I'm proud of the effort you've always given, and I know you'll continue to make that effort." He reminded me that integrity was about doing the right thing and working hard, even when it went unrecognized by others.

It was during those years that I learned an important lesson about myself: what I lacked in speed and natural ability, I made up for with determination and heart. My efforts might go unrewarded by others, but I'd continue to push my limits to prove my abilities to myself. My determination never let me down.

3: THE MAKING OF AN ATHLETE

My college years were an experiment. I spent the first semester away at a small private school in southern Michigan. It wasn't at all what I'd prepared myself for, and it didn't take long for me to realize it wasn't working out. I'd spent high school thinking I wanted to get back to a small-town feel, but by the time I got there, I'd outgrown that.

At the end of my first semester, I packed up my things and went back to East Lansing. There, I checked into a dorm room at Michigan State University, the Big Ten school I'd grown up thinking college was supposed to be.

I loved being a Spartan. That first semester, I loved it a little too much. Academically, I didn't fare well, but I began to find a part of my soul. Over the next few years, I learned how to balance school and freedom, family and friends, but something was still missing.

On an autumn afternoon, I rode my bike from math class to my dorm on the fourth floor of Wilson Hall. It was a Friday. The sun was shining, making the brightly colored leaves sparkle. To my right, the Red Cedar River flowed through campus. I could hear the marching band practicing as they prepared for the football game the next day. They struck up the fight song just as I came around the corner with the huge Sparty statue in full view. I felt goosebumps spread over my skin. I knew I was exactly where I was supposed to be. But I still felt incomplete.

By junior year, I was good friends with several female gymnasts, and my roommate, Britta, was a member of the MSU swim team. I watched them all go off to practice every day, and I realized how much I missed being part of a team.

During the first week of my fourth year at MSU, I loaded up my backpack and was riding my bike to class when someone standing on the sidewalk of Farm Lane in front of Bessie Hall handed me a flier. (Farm Lane, Bessie Hall—yes, I went to an agricultural school, although that wasn't my area of study.) I grabbed the flier as I sped past. Even as I did that, I thought it odd, because I never took fliers. I glanced at it as I pedaled onward. It was an invitation to try out for the rowing team.

"Rowing. Huh," I thought. It sounded interesting, and I considered giving it a shot.

When I arrived home later that afternoon at my little house on Durand Street, my two roommates were already there.

"Hey, you guys," I said, "I got this flier today about the rowing team."

"Oh yeah, I got one, too," they both said.

"I'm thinking about checking it out," I told them. We all agreed to sign up.

It was a somewhat grueling week of try-outs before Coach Matt made an announcement of the new additions to the team. He had us do drills and run. We learned proper technique on the "erg," short for ergometer, the fancy word for rowing machine. At the end of the next week, to be considered for the team, we had to pull two thousand meters on the erg in under nine minutes, a daunting task to us rookies.

The final posting of team members made for some interesting dynamics at our house. One roommate stayed on as a coxswain, the other roommate didn't make the team at all, and I proved myself worthy of being a rower. It was tense at times, but as the year progressed, we all settled into our new routine. I was ecstatic to be part of a team again, even if it was only for my last year of college.

Extending My Stay

Even at club level, rowing was a demanding sport. To get a two-hour practice in before daily classes meant we had to be at the boat house while it was still dark. We watched a lot of sunrises from the seat of a boat and sat shivering in the cold, wind, rain, and snow on both practice and race days. We worked our butts off, sweated like fiends, and formed lifelong friendships through our shared suffering.

During my senior year, Title IX kicked into effect big time on campus. Michigan State needed to make some adjustments to comply with the ruling that required all schools receiving federal funding to provide fair and equal treatment of the sexes in all areas, including athletics. There were debates and roundtables about how to redistribute funding to open up more money for women's sports, as well as discussions about demoting some of the men's teams to club status to fit the budget. We didn't want to take anything away from the other sports on campus, but obviously we were huge supporters of the concept of elevating women's rowing to varsity status. Just a couple of weeks before my graduation, the announcement came: women's rowing was to receive funding as a varsity sport in the 1997–98 school year.

I was as elated for my teammates and friends that spring as I was for myself. I already had my class ring, emblazoned with 1997 on the side. My family was coming to town to watch me graduate in a few weeks. I had the summer ahead to complete one final class and my internship in foster care and adoption through St. Vincent de Paul in Lansing. I proudly walked into a meeting with my academic adviser, ready to sign off on some paperwork for graduation.

But as she sat scanning my transcript, she caught something. "Ummm, hmmm." Her forehead scrunched in concentration as she pored over my credits from the past eight semesters. "You seem to be missing a math credit that you need for graduation."

I stared at her, my eyes wide. "I thought I didn't need that because—"

"No, I'm pretty certain you do," she interrupted.

We scoured the transcripts I'd transferred from other schools, trying to figure out how the math credit had slipped by. Her final verdict was that I needed another class, one that was offered only in the fall. I wasn't graduating.

I left the office in tears. When I got home, I called my mom, sobbing as I told her about the meeting.

"Well, maybe it's a blessing. Now you can stay another year and be a part of the varsity rowing team," she said matter-of-factly as I sniffled on my end of the line.

But as I sat with that idea for a while, it started growing on me. My mom had planted a seed of opportunity.

A short time later, I received a phone call from my adviser. Apologizing profusely, she told me she'd gone over and over my records and had discovered that, because I was a transfer student, I was grandfathered in on the mysterious math credit. I wasn't missing anything, and I could graduate as originally planned.

By then, I wasn't so sure I wanted to. I had one year of eligibility left at Michigan State. I could use it or lose it. I faced a choice: grab opportunity by the horns and stay young or grow up and be an adult. I knew I had my parents' full support, so I postponed my last class and called my internship supervisor. She supported spreading out my internship hours to the end of the calendar year. And so, I made my decision. Even though I had a class ring that said 1997, I'd wait for my diploma until 1998.

Around that same time, our team qualified for Nationals, to be held in Atlanta's Lake Mead where the 1996 Olympic rowing events had taken place. With minimal club team funds, we drove to Atlanta, where we piled four to five girls into a hotel room. Many of the parents drove to Atlanta to support the team, mine included. They left right after my dad got out of his last meeting of the day, drove through the night, and slept in the family van in the parking lot of our hotel. With my roommates' permission, my parents borrowed my room key to take a shower after we cleared out to spend the rest of the day at Lake Mead.

In our first heat, our Novice 8+ qualified to race in the finals. Mom and Dad waited around to watch me race again that afternoon. We didn't make it to the podium, but we'd competed at Nationals, which was a victory in itself.

What stood out more to me than anything else was that my parents drove to Atlanta, slept in a van, and hung out all day to cheer me on for about five minutes. Then they turned around and drove back to Michigan. They logged all that driving just so they could support me. And it wouldn't be the last time.

The 1997–98 school year was, by far, my favorite. I worked at the internship I'd trained for, went to two hours of class a week, and spent the rest of my time living and breathing my sport. As much effort as it required, I had grown to adore rowing. I was a member of the Women's Varsity Crew Inaugural Team at Michigan State. My family came to every event.

My dad contributed to the team on several levels, supporting the team financially and also serving as one of the sports medicine doctors at our races. In 2000, he was recognized for his contributions and given the opportunity to name one of the boats in the fleet. As a family, we talked about different possibilities, but Dad already knew the boat's name. With two Lindseys on the team, differentiated by our last initials, the boat was named as I had been known: It was the Lindsey J.

Just weeks before I was to be married, I drove home to Michigan for the weekend to attend a race and the boat-naming ceremony. In all the excitement, it was easy for me to hide my reaction to the red flag that had raised its head when my future husband declined to attend with me. He didn't think a boat naming was a big deal.

4: REBIRTH OF A RUNNER

When my college days ended and I held an official diploma that read 1998, I packed up my little blue Plymouth Colt and drove to Chicago, where I took my first grown-up job as a crisis counselor for Youth Outreach Services.

I lived in a tiny studio apartment on the north side of the city. I was only about half a block from the lake path. Since there was nowhere better to run than the Chicago lakefront, I took up running again. I returned to my first passion, and I loved it.

A few years later, after returning from a mission trip to Mexico, I went for a run on the lakefront on an early June morning. I ran six miles that day. Somewhere near Shedd Aquarium I thought, maybe I should run a marathon—just once, to say I'd done it.

When I returned home, I looked up the Chicago Marathon. It was scheduled for the second Saturday in October. At first, I decided to wait until July to register. I wanted to get a few more miles under me before I was ready to commit. But I was too excited to wait. Less than a week later, I was determined and ready to sign up.

I called my dad to tell him about my plan. He said, "Yeah, you can do this. I'll talk you through it." He had coached me through just about everything else in life, so I trusted him with that, too.

My stint as a crisis counselor had been short-lived; the pager sucked the fun out of life in Chicago. I'd moved on to a regular schedule teaching preschool, but at the end of the school year, I left teaching to pursue other opportunities.

I had the summer off, with ample time on my hands, so I ran my long runs on Friday mornings. As the runs got longer and more challenging, my sense of accomplishment after completing them grew as well.

Every Friday, after I completed a distance of fourteen, sixteen, eighteen, or twenty miles, I called my dad to tell him about it. One morning, I called him at work, and his assistant transferred the call to him. He had someone in his office, and as he picked up the phone, I heard him say, "It's my daughter. She's training for a marathon." I could hear the pride in his voice, and it made my heart swell. His words had the same effect as if he'd handed me another Snoopy balloon.

911

In the summer of 2001, my dad and I experienced some of the best bonding of our twenty-six-year relationship. In true Jacobs style, a great deal of our shared interest revolved around sports, and that summer was no exception. Along with coaching me through training for my first marathon, he was using his professional connections to investigate any job opportunities for me at the American Osteopathic Association (AOA), located on Michigan Avenue in Chicago. As the dean of the College of Osteopathic Medicine at Michigan State University, he had a little bit of pull, and he knew the right people.

Since I'd left my job at the beginning of summer, I'd spent most of my time training for the marathon and updating my resume. Dad had taken a sabbatical for a few months that summer and was spending most of his time at the newly acquired family condo on Lake Michigan with my mom. My family had spent many weeks of my childhood at the beach in New Buffalo, Michigan, and my parents had just fulfilled a dream and purchased the condo there about a year before. It was in a perfect location, right between their house in East Lansing and my new home in Chicago. I could pop over for a day or they could come my direction.

In addition, my dad was still the dean even while on sabbatical, so he spent a couple of weeks in Chicago for things like the AOA House of Delegates. One day, after a run by the lake, I finished at the Fairmont Hotel, where he'd left a key for me at the desk so I could shower in his room. Then I met him at the conference, where he introduced me to some of the people in his network. After our work there was done, we grabbed lunch at the Corner Bakery.

The following day we took in a Cubs game at Wrigley Field. Whenever we'd taken family trips to Chicago, we visited Wrigley, but I could count on one hand the number of times it had been just the two of us. It was a rare treat.

Dad and I sat in the upper deck on the first base side. The sun was shining, the sky was blue, and there was a light breeze. We ate hot dogs and peanuts. As always, Dad kept score the old-fashioned way in his program. We sat there as father and daughter, watching America's pastime. I breathed deeply and secured the memory in my heart.

That summer, I interviewed with the AOA. In early September, a few weeks before I was to run my first marathon, I received an offer to join them as manager of physician services. I recall walking on Michigan Avenue with my mom when I got the call from human resources offering me the job. I accepted and was set to start my new gig just days before the marathon, which was still a month away. I was equally excited about my upcoming marathon and my involvement with my dad's profession.

A few days later, on a Tuesday morning, I started my day with my usual routine. I dropped my husband at his office downtown and drove to my customary parking spot by Navy Pier, where I did my training runs. I'd completed the Chicago Half Marathon over the weekend in preparation for my main event. I'd pushed hard in the race, so I planned an easy four miles that morning.

I ran south along the lake past Shedd Aquarium before turning around. As I ran, I noticed that the people sitting in their cars in traffic on Lakeshore Drive all had strange, blank expressions on their faces as they drove past me. I had no idea that, while I was out for that run, the world as we knew it had changed forever.

I arrived back at the car and turned on the radio to the voices of Eric and Kathy, the DJs of the morning show I often listened to. They sounded upset about something, but I had no idea what was going on. I listened intently as I drove toward home. They introduced President Bush, but they cut into his address a few seconds late, so I missed the first line or two. As the president spoke, I knew that something awful and historic had occurred. The few moments until I understood what had happened felt like an eternity. Not one, but two, planes had flown into the World Trade Center in New York City. Our country was under attack.

Like nearly everyone else in America, I spent the rest of the day glued to the TV. I was on the phone with my mom, watching in disbelief as the south tower collapsed into a plume of smoke. We gasped in horror.

The loft my husband and I lived in was on the top floor of an old warehouse that had been renovated. It was a corner unit with floor-to-ceiling windows that looked out over the Chicago River, displaying a stunning view of the city skyline. I made my way from the television to the balcony, taking in the blue sky and the city I loved, acutely aware of the eerie silence due to the grounding of the usual stream of planes to the north flying into O'Hare International Airport. I wondered if my beloved Chicago had been planned for demolition that day. My tears flowed down my cheeks until it seemed I had no more tears left. I mourned the world as it had existed only hours before.

We learned the names of the passengers, the flight crew, those working in the twin towers, and the heroic first responders who rushed to their aid. We heard final messages, learned stories of the victims, and America came together in solidarity. The news reported the names and faces of the evil behind the terror. I refused to learn the names of the people who'd committed such an atrocity. They didn't deserve any place in my memory.

One day at a time, we, as a society, picked up the pieces in an attempt to move forward. One step at a time, I continued my training. I started a new job. Life went on. But my heart, like that of every other American, had been changed forever.

Runners, Take Your Mark!

With less than a week until the marathon, I prepared for the first day of my new job. On a Wednesday morning, two days after my birthday, I dressed in business attire and confidently walked into my new office on Ontario Street, as part of the membership team at the AOA. My primary responsibility was to assist the osteopathic students, interns, and residents. Essentially, I would travel with the association president to the various osteopathic schools around the country to act as a liaison.

That first day began with a tour of the association and introductions to the other employees in my department. We went out to lunch as they welcomed me to the team. After lunch, I entered my new office on the ninth floor that had a window that overlooked Michigan Avenue, set up my voicemail and my computer, and logged into my new email account. The first email I sent was to Al Jacobs, dean of the Michigan State University College of Osteopathic Medicine.

I familiarized myself with my surroundings, glancing frequently out the floor-to-ceiling window that looked out on the Magnificent Mile. I couldn't believe I'd landed a position with such perks.

It wasn't long until I received notice of a new email on my computer. It read:

> Lindsey,
> Congratulations on the new job. Great office, great location, great place to work. I hope you will be able to go to San Diego for annual convention. I am sure you and the others at the AOA will get along well. Tried to talk to you on the phone last night, but it didn't work out. See you Sunday.
> Love, Dad

"Sunday," I thought to myself. Sunday was the marathon. And Dad was going to be there to see it.

As race day neared, Mom realized they were double-booked, scheduled to be in Maryland the night before the marathon. My brother, who played football for the Eastern Michigan Eagles, had a Saturday night game against the University of Connecticut Huskies. Mom and Dad couldn't fly back until Sunday. As Mom explained to Dad, she didn't think they'd make it back in time to see me.

"Lindsey needs us there," he told her. "We *have* to be there." He knew how desperately I needed his support.

Mom had to jump through hoops to make it happen, but she came through. After my brother's game that Saturday night, my parents drove to the hotel next to the airport. A few short hours later, they caught the earliest flight to Chicago Midway.

Marathon morning was a whirlwind. My husband dropped me off near the start, where I joined the herd of other runners. Thousands of us made our way into the corrals.

The weather had been warm right up until race day, but the temperature plummeted overnight, prompting a last-minute wardrobe change due to the cold. The temperature hovered around freezing at the start and was predicted to warm up to around fifty degrees. I chose silver tights and a long-sleeve green and white jersey from my rowing days at Michigan State, topped off with a Cubs bandana wrapped around my head to contain my dripping sweat and declare my loyalty. I'd taken Dad's advice. Rather than wearing gloves I might not want after the sun rose and warmed the air, I grabbed an old pair of socks to put on my hands. I didn't feel bad about tossing an old pair of socks as I ran if I no longer needed them.

Anticipation and adrenaline overflowed as start time neared. Nervous energy floated through the air; runners chatted excitedly. I was positioned in a corral near the back of the pack.

It was my first marathon, and I didn't have much to go on other than a rough estimate of how long it would take me to run 26.2 miles. I was surrounded by a group of runners in monkey suits, someone wearing a huge Eiffel Tower that appeared extremely heavy, and several runners toting American flags in support of our country following the tragic events of September.

After the national anthem, we heard the gun signal the start, and we inched our way forward. There were so many people between me and the start line, it took me a solid fifteen minutes to reach it.

I felt as if I were floating as I passed through the giant arch indicating the beginning of my twenty-six-mile journey. My adrenaline pumped; I fought the urge to take off in a dead sprint. But I thought of my dad's lessons on pacing: "When you've got a long way to go, you don't want to burn all your fuel right out the gate. Set a comfortable pace so you have enough left at the end. If you have anything left over, leave it all on the course. But you've got to get there first. The end goal is going the distance."

Upon their arrival in Chicago, my mom and dad had no idea where I was on the course. I didn't carry the flip phone I shared with my husband. Instead, he had it to contact my parents. After their flight landed, they called him to find out where they might have the best shot at seeing me. Race technology of timing chips and runner tracking was in the very early stages, and the updates spectators could access were unreliable at best. So my parents took their best guess according to the time I'd started and the pace I'd consistently trained at. They made their way toward State Street in downtown Chicago in hopes of finding me somewhere near the halfway point.

The course wound through the streets of downtown before heading north along the lake, up through the neighborhood I'd lived in for a year between my first apartment and buying our first married home. From there, we continued north up to Belmont where we turned west and ran a short distance before turning back south and aiming toward downtown.

I ran south on Clark Street; I'd not seen any of my friends who said they'd be out spectating. I knew there'd be a lot of people, but nothing could have prepared me for the huge number of spectators. People stood four to five deep on either side of the street that was packed with runners bobbing up and down as far as I could see. I wondered how in the world I'd spot my family when I didn't know where to look for them or if they'd even arrived in Chicago yet.

We ran through Old Town and made our way back into the Loop. As we approached the halfway point of the race, I felt miserable. I was tired, and my feet hurt. I felt a blister that had rubbed on my toe; I was sure it was bleeding. As the horde plodded along the downtown streets lined with skyscrapers, I hung my head and stared at my Adidas. I began to pray, "God, this is horrible. I really don't want to be doing this anymore. I need a familiar face right now."

At that exact moment, I lifted my head and I looked past the four street lanes full of other runners to the spectators on the far side of the street in front of Marshall Fields. It was as if a light shone down from heaven onto the face of one spectator. He was standing amid the masses, trying to catch a glimpse of the runners as they passed. It was my dad.

I darted across the street that was packed like a sardine can, almost tripping other runners in the process, but I didn't care. After twelve-plus miles, we hadn't spread out much. I swam cross-stream and reached the other side, jumping up and down in front of my parents. They were looking past me, still scanning the sea of runners.

"I'm here," I shouted at them. "I'm right here!" Their shocked expressions gave way to huge smiles. They couldn't believe that instead of their spotting me, I'd found them. After quick high fives, I continued my run down State Street.

At the sight of Mom and Dad, my emotions took over. Suppressing the tears that filled my eyes and the lump that formed in my throat, I started to hyperventilate. I took a couple deep breaths to shake it off, and the wheezing subsided. I marveled at the gift of that one brief moment.

I spent the rest of the marathon looking for my dad's face, but I never saw it again on the course. I looked for my cousin Doug among the runners and his brother's family along with my aunt and grandma, knowing they were out there cheering us both on. I was fairly certain Doug was way ahead of me, as this wasn't his first rodeo. Somewhere in Chinatown, I found my husband and his parents, who cheered me on and handed me a few bites of a ham and cheese sandwich. From there, we ran south to Comiskey Park, home of the White Sox, before turning north for the long run up Michigan Avenue to the finish.

In any marathon, there are a few miles known by runners as "hitting the wall." After putting one foot in front of the other for twenty miles, many people were struggling, hitting the wall. On South Michigan Avenue, hundreds of athletes walked along the stretch back to Grant Park. Runners who'd given up were scattered along the sides, sitting on the curb. Others stretched tight calf muscles or hamstrings that had seized from overuse. But I continued my slow, relentless forward progress, shuffling toward the finish in my refusal to quit. As I climbed the only hill on the Chicago Marathon course, the final challenge before the end, I reached deep down inside of myself and willed my body to give anything it had left. I cruised the final hundred meters lined with yelling spectators, smiling broadly, basking in the joy that I'd made it.

I crossed that finish line with an explosion of emotion, elated that I'd accomplished my goal. I'd poured out my whole self; I was depleted. My toe throbbed, and I wanted nothing more than to take off my shoe. A volunteer draped a silver mylar wrap around my shoulders as another placed a finisher's medal around my neck.

"Congratulations!" she said.

"Thanks." I gave her a tired smile and limped off to locate my fan club.

We'd wisely established a meeting spot for all of us to find each other after the race. I wasn't sure why I'd picked Buckingham Fountain, other than it was easy to find. In my exhaustion, getting to it seemed equivalent to climbing Mt. Everest, as I hobbled across Grant Park. I slowly made my way to the steps between Buckingham Fountain and Lakeshore Drive, and there they were. My family. My dad. Despite all the obstacles, he was there to congratulate me at the finish of my first marathon.

They saw me limp toward them and rushed to greet me with hugs and smiles. We marked the moment with photos, the blue sky shining over the skyline in the background. I sat down on the steps in front of the fountain to remove my shoes, revealing a blood-stained sock. I'd pushed through the pain in my toe, the pain throughout my body, and the mental fatigue. I had proof of the blood, sweat, and tears it took to complete a full marathon.

As I rode the high of the moment, my body started to cool down and crave real calories. Dad left to bring the car around. When he returned, he pulled up onto the sidewalk in front of the famous fountain and opened the door like a chauffeur for me to get in. I felt like royalty in his presence once again.

Once home, I couldn't wait to peel off the sweaty layers, take a long, hot shower, and eat a sandwich. Even with my family around me, I spent the afternoon mostly curled up in fetal position or asleep. I lay in bed in our loft overlooking the Chicago River with a view of the city skyline and heard my grandma ask, "Where did Lindsey go?"

I didn't have the energy to answer.

5: TOO MANY LOSSES

After working in my new position for a couple weeks, I traveled to San Diego for the annual convention. Then I began my travels with the president for his visits to the osteopathic schools.

Our first school visit was to Michigan State University College of Osteopathic Medicine, where my dad was the dean. After being picked up from the Lansing airport by my mom, I spent Halloween evening at my parents' house eating my mom's homemade chili. It most definitely did not feel like a business trip.

The morning of our meeting, I got ready and rode to the office with Dad. Once at the school, we met with President Zini, among others, in Dad's office before going to greet the students. My dad introduced each of us to the several hundred students who filled the lecture hall.

When Dad came to me, he said, "Lindsey is your AOA representative. She's here to answer all your questions. And she just happens to be my daughter." We could all see the pride as it oozed out of him. I couldn't have loved my job more than I did at that moment.

Growing up, I worked many hours during the summer in the clinic, helping Dad with sports medicine physicals. I also worked in his office, organized his books and slides, ran errands, and did whatever else was needed. I felt very much at home in both the medical and academic settings, especially the combination of both.

Later that month, we reconvened in Saint Louis for National Osteopathic Medicine Week. We attended meetings by day and fun group activities by night. After dinner one evening, Dad and I sat in his hotel room watching TV.

"Hey, Dad, there's something I've been wanting to talk to you about," I broached.

"Yeah, what's up?" He grabbed the remote to turn down the volume.

"Well, being at all the osteopathic schools kinda has me thinking. I've done some research, and I think I want to go to med school."

"That's fantastic."

"I know it won't be easy since I need to get some pre-reqs out of the way before I can even apply. But I've got some options with schools in Chicago that offer night classes." I told him about all I'd investigated.

"I know you can do it, Lindsey. I'll help you with whatever I can." I knew Dad meant it, and I was glad I'd shared my thoughts with him.

When I got up from the sofa to go back to my room, he hugged me good night at the door. "I'm really proud of you," he said. "With your determination, you can do anything."

The next day, Dad had to fly home to Michigan, but I stayed in Saint Louis for another night to attend the foundation gala. Dad had asked me if I could drive him to the airport, but I needed to stick around for the meetings that afternoon to finish up some business.

As Dad prepared to leave, we said goodbye in the hallway outside the Saint Louis Union Station conference rooms. Our conversation from the previous night was still fresh in my mind. I could already picture him on stage with me at the hooding ceremony.

Dad wore the green suede sportscoat he was so fond of. As I hugged him goodbye, I felt a pull in my heart. I chalked it up to wishing I could drive him to the airport. A lump rose up in my throat as I lifted my hand to touch the softness of his jacket. I would later understand that the pull I felt was my heart holding on to every detail about that moment.

"Bye, Dad," I said, letting my hand drop. He readjusted the strap of his bag over his shoulder and raised his hand in a wave. I watched him walk a few steps, then took a deep breath and pushed open the heavy conference room door. Back to work.

A week or so later, it was a typical Wednesday night in November. I'd been out with several girlfriends from church and was driving south on Western Avenue, headed home.

I grabbed my phone and punched in my parents' number on speed dial.

"Hello?" Dad answered.

"Hey, Dad."

"Hello," he said again as a sincere greeting, rather than a question.

We talked for a few minutes, sharing updates on the happenings of life and our plans for the weekend. He was going to the MSU basketball game on Saturday night with my brother. I was flying to Florida on Sunday to meet President Zini for a Monday meeting at one of the schools.

As our conversation wound down, I said, "Well, I guess I'll let you go."

"Good talking to you. Love you."

"I love you, too, Dad."

A couple nights later, I packed for a visit to the osteopathic school in Fort Lauderdale. I eagerly anticipated the Florida temperatures, as late November always brought cold and gray to Chicago. I threw a swimsuit in my suitcase, just in case.

Setting an alarm for the flight the next morning, I climbed into bed and drifted off to sleep. I was dreaming of the sunshine I'd be enjoying in just a few hours when my dreams were disturbed by the phone ringing at two o'clock in the morning.

My husband answered groggily and then handed the phone to me. I knew whatever news awaited on the other end, it wasn't good.

"Hello?" I said sleepily.

"Lindsey . . ." I heard my mom's voice.

I waited.

"It's your dad."

"Yeah?"

"He's gone."

"I know." Somehow, before she'd said the words, I'd felt it in my heart.

Mom continued talking, telling me the details of what had happened to Dad.

". . . heart attack . . . really fast . . . CPR . . . ambulance . . . Sparrow Hospital . . ."

I was sitting on the bed with the phone in my hand, listening to her voice. But I was also standing on the other side of the room, watching myself try to process the jumble of words and the horror of what had happened.

It was a heart attack. The same thing that had taken my grandpa at forty-four years old had stolen my dad at fifty-nine. While I understood the words, my brain couldn't—or didn't want to—grasp that my dad had died. My own heart felt as if it had been ripped straight from my chest; my head was spinning and foggy.

Time seemed to rewind and flood backward in my mind. I saw the image of my dad in his green suede jacket. The last words I'd said to him, "I love you, too, Dad," echoed in my brain. I flashed back to that hug in the hotel room, "I'm really proud of you." I tried to comprehend a strange new world without my life coach.

Trouble in Paradise

I'd been married only a little over a year, and my dad was suddenly gone. Carrying on his legacy seemed more important than ever, and suddenly, I felt desperate to have a baby. The plan to go to med school fell by the wayside. It resurfaced in my brain periodically, but family became my new priority.

A few years into our marriage, I gave birth to a beautiful baby girl. We named her Ally in honor of my dad, Al, whom I missed so much.

I loved being a mom so much that I quit my job to stay home with Ally full time. Twenty-seven months later, on my dad's birthday, Ally gained a brother. And twenty-seven months after that, Ally's second brother was born.

Thoughts of medical school came and went, but after a few years, I lacked the confidence I'd once had. I doubted that I possessed the ability to tackle a challenge of such magnitude. I no longer believed I was capable of anything more than being a wife and a mom. But I could still run marathons—at least when I wasn't consumed with guilt for doing something that made me uniquely me.

I had three beautiful, healthy children, and I spent my days taking care of them. We took amazing family vacations to Hawaii, Disney World, and the Bahamas. I lived in a beautifully rehabbed house in the heart of Lincoln Park, and I trained for marathons on the Chicago lakefront. What more could I possibly ask for?

But the fits of rage, the blame game, and my husband's ability to make me feel as if everything in the world was my fault were just a few of the things I'd swept under the rug from the start of our marriage. As time went on, I became more and more afraid to use my voice. I got quieter and quieter, until, eventually, I stopped talking and climbed inside myself. My husband invalidated my feelings and ignored my opinions. I felt invisible and insignificant.

On a trip to the Bahamas in February 2010, we got off the plane and saw a banner promoting the Bahamas Marathon and Half-Marathon. I wasn't trained for a full marathon, but I could certainly manage a half. After running the Detroit Marathon in the fall of 2009, I'd kept my mileage up for such opportunities. I thought about how cool it would be to explore the island in a way I otherwise wouldn't have attempted.

After we checked in at the hotel, I looked at the race website and found I could register at the race expo. The day before the race, we visited the Atlantis Resort, where the expo was held to explore and sign up.

I was so excited I could hardly contain myself. I could get up early, go run, and still be back not long after the kids awoke to celebrate Ally's birthday. Or, since the course went right by the hotel, perhaps my husband would bring the kids downstairs to cheer me on as I ran by. He rarely brought them to see me race, but I was hopeful.

As we left the expo, my husband said to me, "You owe me for this one." He intended to sound playful, but I knew he meant it.

"Oh, I know. I know I do!" I responded. And I believed what I said. I felt I had to earn the opportunity to do things for myself or return the favor, so to speak. I didn't think I was allowed to participate in the activities that made me *Me* unless I received his permission or promised to erase another little part of my soul to become the person he expected me to be.

The next morning, I joined several hundred other runners gathered at the start line. It was a small race. I didn't have my race watch, since I'd figured I would run on a treadmill at the hotel, if at all.

The race started, and I set out to see the sights of the island and enjoy myself. As I approached the hotel a few miles into the race, I looked toward the circle drive, but I saw only a bellman and a taxi driver, who looked up as I went by. I glanced toward the direction of the room I knew my kids were in, hoping to see their little faces pressed against the window. Just curtains. I felt my heart sink, as it had so many times before, but I brushed my disappointment aside and continued running along the coast. It was a beautiful course.

I noted the clock time as I passed through the finish. Not my best, but not my worst. I gathered my new race bling before walking the few blocks back to the hotel.

When I arrived at our room, the kids didn't care about my sweaty, salty clothes, and they charged me with hugs. But I could feel the tension that hung in the air. It was as if I was being punished for leaving the family vacation for a couple hours to race. I allowed my husband to make me feel small, to make my ambitions feel small. I realized my wants and needs were insignificant compared to those of the person who was supposed to be my partner.

Increasingly, he piled on the guilt and minimized my strengths until I no longer felt loved or cared for. He told me so often that I shouldn't feel a certain way that I no longer knew how to feel anything at all. My opinions, which hadn't carried much weight at any point in our relationship, now seemed completely void. I continued down a path toward total emotional numbness.

An Official Announcement

The first time I made the announcement that I no longer loved my husband and was totally unsatisfied in our marriage was in April of 2009. I knew that by saying it out loud, I was risking everything. I had three small children, and I was a stay-at-home mom with no income of my own. But I needed to tell him how I felt in order to save myself. There was no other option. It felt like an out-of-body experience as I said the words to him. He was furious at me. How could I do this to him?

Shortly after our argument began, he left and went to his sister's house for the night, saying he said he needed space. That seemed ironic, considering that one of my biggest complaints was I so often felt alone in raising our kids, but I was rarely allowed to take time or space for myself.

The next day, he called me from work. He was coming home to gather some things and get on a train to Saint Louis immediately. His mother had been admitted to the hospital with bacterial meningitis. I would stay in Chicago with the kids, and we'd figure things out as more information came. Nothing like a family emergency to defuse a marital explosion, I thought. His mom was in the hospital for a week or so but continued to improve and was eventually released to recover at home.

Shortly after this blowup, we began marriage counseling. While it seemed to help on the surface, in reality, I didn't feel safe enough to say any of what was going on inside of me. I continued to do my best to put on my happy face, go through the motions, and pretend things were fine when I was actually escaping to a dream world at every opportunity. Even running became more of an unhealthy addiction than a healthy habit. I was running away from reality. I was chasing a fantasy.

Another Jolting Loss

Over the summer of 2010, we put our Lincoln Park house on the market for the third time. We'd tried to sell the previous year, but it hadn't panned out. The idea was, if it sold, we'd move to Saint Louis to be closer to my husband's family. The kids could have multigenerational influence and more time with their cousins.

After a few hiccups, the house finally sold, and in mid-September, we packed up the life we'd built in Chicago and took it south on Interstate 55 to Saint Louis. We landed in my husband's parents' house for a couple months while we sorted out the short sale we were interested in a few miles down the road.

In early October, the kids started in their new school. My husband still traveled a lot, and I filled my time getting adjusted to a new life. The closing date set for October 29 fell through, and we had to wait a couple more weeks. I was frustrated but ultimately grateful for the delay.

The next day, a Friday, the kids were off school, so we went off to the dollar store so they could pick out items to fill shoeboxes for Operation Christmas Child. As we drove toward Lifetime Fitness, where I'd exercise for a while, my mom called. We talked for a few minutes, and as I pulled into the parking lot, she said goodbye to take another call and she hung up to answer it. I dropped the kids off at the Kids Klub and went upstairs to jump on an elliptical.

About halfway through my workout, my husband unexpectedly appeared in front of me. I pulled out my earbud and looked at him quizzically.

"I need you to come outside with me," he said.

I was confused. I wondered if he'd bought a new car to surprise me, or if he had bad news. I tried to read his blank expression as I followed him down the stairs and outside.

We exited the building into the October sunshine, and he said, "Your mom called. Sunshyne died this morning."

I stared at him. His words didn't make any sense. I'd just talked to my mom, and everything had been fine. My brother's wife, Sunshyne, had just turned thirty and was pregnant with their second child. She couldn't have died.

I felt as if all the air was sucked out of my lungs, and with it, the words, "Oh, my brother . . ." escaped my lips almost inaudibly.

He tried to pull me to him in a hug, but my arms hung against my sides.

"I need to sit down," I said. I opened the door to go back inside and was looking for somewhere to sit, but he kept trying to pull me the other way.

"I need to sit down—now," I said, trying to make him release me.

I was on the verge of passing out, so I did the only thing I could. I sat down right there, on the floor of the Lifetime lobby. I wanted to cry. I wanted to scream and throw things. But I felt numb, totally trapped inside myself. I thought I was sad or angry, but I wasn't really sure what I was supposed to feel because of shock. And because everything about my life was so controlled by someone else, I'd lost my ability to know.

That night, I boarded a plane to Los Angeles. No other flight in my life was ever so long. My husband came with me; the kids stayed with his parents. By the time I found my way to my brother, it was after two o'clock in the morning. He was awake, lying in bed in an upstairs room at his friend Chris's house. I climbed into the bed and curled myself around him. It was safe to feel again, and I knew I needed to start doing that.

It was an emotional and exhausting week, planning a funeral for a young, vibrant woman and my unborn nephew. Despite trips to the doctor and the ER, Sunshyne had succumbed to an undiagnosed blood clot that had bothered her for several days. That morning when she'd heard their eighteen-month-old daughter crying, she'd brought the toddler back to their bedroom. She laid her down on the bed with my brother, looked at him, and gasped the words, "I can't breathe—." Then she collapsed.

The funeral was scheduled for Thursday. My husband flew to Texas for a deposition on Wednesday. As much as it irritated me that he didn't stay, there was a larger part of me that neither cared nor really wanted him there. When he wasn't around, it was safe for me to feel. That's when I could finally breathe.

The next day, I returned to my babies in Saint Louis. My body was wracked with grief, and I needed to see my kids. Ironically, I was flying back to Saint Louis at the same time I was supposed to fly from Saint Louis to New York City. It was the weekend of the New York City Marathon, which I'd looked forward to for months. I cancelled my hotel and my flight, intending to defer my marathon registration to the following year.

Once I was back in Saint Louis, another running opportunity presented itself. I pled my case to my husband so I could return to LA two weeks later. My sister-in-law had been registered for the Malibu Half-Marathon, and I wanted to run in her honor.

I was trained for a full marathon, so I opted to go for it. I'd run the Chicago Marathon in early October and had prepared to run NYC the previous week, so by training standards, my body was in shape. What I wasn't prepared for, though, was the toll the previous weeks had taken on my body. I was drained before the race even started.

The heat, the wind blowing in from the ocean, the hills of the Pacific Coast Highway—any of these would have been tough enough to contend with on their own. But the presence of my mom, my brother, and my niece on the course supporting me counteracted them. I listened to some of Sunshyne's favorite songs on my iPod and watched dolphins play in the waves. Those things carried me through a tough 26.2 miles.

With a couple hundred meters to go, a song that made me think of Sunshyne, a reminder to rejoice in all circumstances, piped through my headphones. Tears flowed freely from my eyes, and I was sobbing as I entered the finishers' chute.

A woman on the sideline yelled, "It's okay. You made it. You're almost there."

I wanted to tell her, "You have no idea what you're talking about, lady. You have absolutely no idea."

As I crossed the finish, I blew a kiss to heaven for my dad, as I'd done at the end of every race since my second marathon. And then I sent up two more kisses.

Something unique about the Malibu Marathon is that rather than giving out a finisher's T-shirt, they gave us beach towels. After ending right on the beach, I removed my shoes and waded out into the ocean. The cold water refreshed me and eased my weary feet. I knew my soul needed to be refreshed as well, but I didn't know how or even what that would look like.

Some of my brother's good friends lived nearby in Malibu. We went to their place so I could shower and relax for a bit before we all went out to eat. While we were there, I checked my phone for the photos I'd taken along the way. One photo struck me. I didn't even remember taking it.

I said, "Whoa, you guys, look at this photo I took. You won't believe it."

It was a photo of the three of them: Mom, my niece Brooke, and my brother AJ, standing on a cliff that overlooked the ocean. They held a sign that read "Lindsey J Running for Sunshyne." But the most beautiful part was the three beams of sun shining down, touching each of their shoulders.

We all stared at it in awe.

That night I caught a red-eye flight to Saint Louis and landed with enough time to go straight to the closing on our new house. The next day, we began moving our belongings from my husband's parents' house into the new house. At the same time, I was beginning to process some realizations I'd had since Sunshyne's death.

Nothing in life was promised; life could end abruptly. It was clear I was unhappy with my own life, but I couldn't put my finger on why. I had everything, or so it seemed to the outside world, but something vital was missing.

Losing my sister-in-law had stirred emotions in me that had died with my dad a decade before. It was time for me to start taking a look inside and figure out what I wanted from my life. I needed to rediscover who I was and what defined me, because I'd attached my identity to my husband. I was letting him call all the shots, and it wasn't working anymore.

6: BOTTOMING OUT

"I don't cry," I declared to Jen, my new counselor. "I just . . . can't."

I sat cross-legged on the loveseat in Jen's office, my arms wrapped around a pillow. *Loveseat* seemed the wrong term, because I didn't love being there, nor did I love the idea of talking about what had brought me to Jen. But it was clear to me that this was where I needed to be.

I wore what had become my standard daily attire: ripped jeans and black Converse shoes, a T-shirt, and a gray cap pulled down over my face to keep it hidden. I was mired in shame, so I dressed the part.

I'd found Jen at New Hope Counseling on the recommendation of my good friend Lynn from my life in Chicago, who'd grown up in Saint Louis. A few weeks prior, I'd left Lynn a rambling voicemail that ultimately led to my asking if her mom, who was a counselor, could suggest someone for me to talk to about the baggage I was carting around.

"I mean, other than at the end of a race," I told Jen, "sometimes I feel like I could, ya know, cry. Kind of like I want to but then it just disappears. I go, uh . . . numb. It's like I've forgotten how. Does that even make sense?"

"Uh-huh," Jen nodded. "So, what do you want to talk about?"

I spent the next forty-five minutes going through my dad dying, my sister-in-law dying, leaving my friends in Chicago, and moving to Saint Louis where I knew almost no one. I touched on the stress of being a stay-at-home mom with a husband who traveled a lot and being in a marriage that made me feel frustrated and small, though I really didn't understand why.

The words tumbled out of me, spewing forth so fast I couldn't have stopped them if I'd tried. I stared over Jen's shoulder out the window at the darkening sky as I continued. I could hear my own unhappiness, but I kept returning to the theme that I really should be grateful because I had so much. I had a husband who provided for me and the kids, we had a large house with a newly renovated kitchen, and we went on amazing vacations. But I felt as if something was missing. I lacked peace in my soul. I lacked contentment. I felt restless and uneasy. I felt as if I always had to put on a happy face and pretend that I wasn't miserable.

When I finally stopped talking to take a breath, I saw that Jen was studying me. It felt uncomfortable for someone to look at me and really see me, to listen to me and not only pay attention to the words I was saying but actually hear them. Words that weren't pretty and flowery. Words that were about pain, difficulties, and struggles, even as trivial as some of them sounded when I spoke them out loud.

"Lindsey," she said, "any one of the many things you just told me would be a good reason for you to be here. That's a lot to unpack. You have a lot going on inside you, and I think we're going to be at this for a while."

I stared at her in disbelief. She hadn't told me it was all nothing and I should just get over it. She hadn't told me I was silly or ungrateful for being unhappy. Validating my feelings was not at all what I'd expected her to do, so I took a deep breath and nodded in agreement.

There were so many things I hadn't even touched on in that first hour session with Jen, secrets I'd locked away in the darkest parts of my memory. I couldn't yet comprehend the way some things had wreaked havoc on my heart and mind. But we were on our way, beginning to peel back the layers of the onion that was the grief I'd tried to bury. We set a time for our next meeting.

For years, I sat on Jen's couch at least once a week. I rarely missed a session. Every so often, if I couldn't make it there, we'd do a phone call instead, during which I'd imagine her sitting in her chair at the desk in her cozy office. When my life circumstances got really bad, we sometimes had an emergency session.

There were times I looked forward to being there in the security of Jen's office, which had become my safe place, and times I dreaded going, knowing I needed to talk about things that were uncomfortable and ugly. But those, I came to understand, were the times I needed to be there most. It was hard, but I continued to show up and do the work.

Jen walked with me through one season after another. Sometimes I yelled or swore. After a few months of seeing Jen regularly, I was able to release those tears I'd wrongly assumed were locked inside me forever. There were even times I barely made it up the stairs and through the door to Jen's office before sinking into the couch in a puddle of tears. The girl who couldn't cry had become a full-blown crier. I shared all kinds of tears in Jen's office—sad, angry, anxious, and afraid. But we had to dive in and find them first.

Downward Spiral

The few months after Sunshyne died were a blur. I threw myself headfirst into running, which seemed like the only thing I had any control over. I was so lonely. I had a husband who traveled most of the week while I raised our kids in a community where I knew almost no one. I was ecstatic to reconnect with an ex-boyfriend from my younger days who lived across the river. He was also a runner, so he provided me with tips on good places to run, helped me when I wasn't sure whom to call, and listened to my frustrations.

I alternated between a desire to come to grips with reality and a need to escape it entirely. I was in limbo; my uncertainty was eating me alive. All the while, I was training for the Nashville Marathon and was on pace to qualify for Boston.

All that came to a screeching halt at the beginning of April 2011. In the early-morning hours of April 2, my marriage came crashing down around me.

The previous evening, my husband had some guys over to play a friendly game of poker. I tucked the boys in their beds, then Ally and I curled up in the king-size master bed to watch a movie. She snuggled next to me, but I wasn't mentally there. My mind swirled all over the place. It was time to confess my secret.

When the movie ended, I put Ally to bed and sat in our room, waiting. Waiting for the guys to leave, waiting to be kicked out of the house, waiting for my life to come to an end.

Shortly after midnight, my husband opened the bedroom door, surprised to see me still awake.

His puzzled look quickly turned to fear as I said, "I have something I need to tell you."

I confessed to him that during the past many months, while I'd been trying to understand my own misery with life, I'd found a means of escape. My coping mechanism had turned into a full-blown affair.

He stared at me, shocked. "What?" he asked.

Even as I formed the words, I had a hard time believing I was saying them. "I've fallen in love with someone else. I can't do this anymore."

He fell to the floor, hands over his face, and began sobbing. I felt as if I'd been deservedly punched in the stomach.

"Who all knows about this?" he asked between sobs.

"No one," I answered truthfully. I hadn't told a living soul until that moment.

"Are you leaving me?"

"He's staying with his wife and family. She was threatening to reveal our affair to you, so I needed to tell you myself."

"But . . . where does that leave us?"

"I don't know. I just know it can't stay how it is."

"I need to get out of here," he said. "I'm going to my parents' house."

"Are you sure you should drive right now?" I asked. But I knew I couldn't stop him, and his parents lived just down the road.

I spent the whole night unable to sleep. Just as I started to drift off, the phone rang, and I heard his cries of "Why? I love you. How could you do this to me?"

I wrestled with his words. He said he loved me, but his words were a bitter contrast to my experience. My truth was that he didn't really want me; he simply didn't want to lose me. I struggled through the night until finally the dark sky gave way to the sun. It was a beautiful spring day, which only seemed to highlight how dark I felt inside.

He came home and packed up the kids to take them to his parents' house. I kissed their confused little faces as they wondered why mommy was staying home alone instead of going along with them. I spent the better part of that day hidden under the covers. Occasionally, I emerged to field phone calls from all the people he'd notified throughout the night and into the morning: the counselor we'd seen back in Chicago, various friends and family members, my two best friends in the world, my brother, my mom, everyone. Everyone now knew of my shame.

He took me to the church and told the pastors. He drove me over to the small private school our kids attended, where I confessed to the head of school and the kids' teachers. I spent the next month feeling as if I wore a huge scarlet *A* on my chest.

My desire to go anywhere or do anything disappeared. He allowed me to take my kids to school and pick them up. If I strayed anywhere off the beaten path, I had to check in constantly so he knew my whereabouts. He required me to keep my phone unlocked and to hand it over whenever he requested. I turned over all my passwords, and he questioned me about every one of my friends on Facebook. I was stripped of privacy and dignity and clothed in stripes of shame and guilt.

Running was over. Eating was over. I spent most days lying in bed or on the couch with a blanket over my head. He had canceled his travels and was working from home indefinitely. We went to counseling several times a week. The only place I was allowed to drive myself was to Jen's office. I was never alone, but I felt more alone than I ever had in my life. I was in emotional isolation, solitary confinement.

Most days looked the same. One day, however, I sat on the kitchen counter, ankles crossed, while he made a sandwich. We were having a regular conversation when out of the blue I said, "Well, you know what happened when I was younger."

He raised his eyebrows at me. "Um, noooooo," he answered, the *o* trailing on and then falling into the abyss. "What are you talking about?"

I uncrossed my legs and let them dangle from the counter. I tucked my hands under my knees, and I realized that maybe the ugly thing wasn't written all over me.

I proceeded to cautiously relate parts of the thing I'd never shared with anyone. It puzzled me to discover that the skeleton I'd dragged around for nearly twenty-five years was, in fact, invisible to everyone but me. But I'd just let the cat out of the bag, and it was time to either face it or shove it back in the closet even deeper than before.

I'm four years old, standing on the ladder of the diving board, waiting for my turn to jump. I've jumped from the side of the pool before, but as I slowly edge nearer to the end of the board, I wonder how it suddenly got so much higher. My toes find the end of the board, and I lean to peer over the edge. As I stare into the depths of the blue-tinted water, I'm certain I see a shape down near the drain. I try to focus my eyes, even though the kids squirming behind me in line are getting antsy waiting for their chance on the board. I bore my eyes into the deep, convinced I see something down there. But it's not something. It's some*one*.

I point to the bottom of the pool and in a shaky voice tell the lifeguard, "I think there's someone down there." He looks beneath him but doesn't see anything of concern.

He attempts to assuage my fear of the diving board by assuring me, "It's only your shadow." I gaze at the shape on the bottom and ask, "But why is she bigger than me?"

"The sun is stretching your shadow," says the lanky teenager in the lifeguard chair. "It's okay."

I wonder why the shadow appears to have darker skin. Well, it is a shadow. But why does it look like my shadow is wearing a yellow swimsuit when I'm clearly wearing blue?

From behind me in line, I hear the irritated voice of an older kid say, "Come ooonnnn!"

I'm so conflicted. I question my gut instinct. I must be wrong. I prepare to jump. I take a big gulp to fill my little lungs with air and cautiously fling myself off the board. After hitting the water, I'm determined to get a better look. I try to go deep enough to see but not so deep I'll get dragged to the bottom if there is someone down there. It's terrifying.

I open my eyes, feeling the burn of chlorine, and, sure enough, there's a lifeless body on the bottom of the pool, wearing a yellow swimsuit. Her black hair moves in the sway of the water. I kick my little four-year-old legs with all my might and reach for the surface for what feels like an eternity before finally breaking through to suck in the air. The lifeguard in the water grabs my wrist and pulls me toward the ladder. I gasp and pant as I desperately cling to the side of the pool. Someone else is standing at the end of the board. getting ready to jump.

Rapidly trying to catch my breath, I insist to the lifeguard at the side, "There is someone down there!" He looks and considers the shape at the bottom. He blows the whistle, grabbing everyone's attention. The commotion ceases; he jumps in.

There's a gap in the memory. The next thing I see is a girl a little older than myself, black skin, yellow swimsuit, lying on the concrete pool deck while several lifeguards pump her body and try to breathe life into her. I wonder if they should be doing that on the concrete, worried they'll hurt her.

Another gap in the memory.

Then I'm walking to the parking lot with my mom's hand around mine. I see an ambulance in the distance at the gate, siren off but red and blue lights flashing. They push a stretcher into the back, carrying the girl in the yellow swimsuit.

"Yes," I think in my innocence and naivety, "she should go to the hospital, and the doctors will make it all better."

End of memory.

Finally, that memory became clear. Memories are funny; they can get so blurry you aren't sure if they actually happened or not. Was it a dream? Had I made that up in my mind from something I'd seen on TV? But at the same time, memories can be so vivid, so real.

I'd thought about that little girl on the bottom of the pool often over the years. I'd never thought to ask my mom, who'd been at the pool with me that day, if what happened was real or imagined. Or maybe I didn't want to know. If I didn't ask, then I could write the story the way I wanted to.

Finally, three decades later, I mentioned it out of the blue. Mom stared at me in astonishment and said, "I can't believe you remember that!"

After all those years, I asked what had happened to the little girl on the bottom of the pool. In my mind, in my optimism, I'd created a scenario in which they pulled her out, cleared her lungs, and she went on to live a happy life.

Sadly, my mom informed me, the happy ending I'd written was not the reality that played out. So many years later, I found myself grieving a little black girl in a yellow swimsuit whom I never knew and who I thought existed only in my dreams. I wondered about her family and what her life would have been like if the lifeguard had believed me sooner.

Even though I'd written the story differently in my mind than the way it played out in real life, it was a lot for a child to take on, to process, and to carry around all those years. I suppose it made sense that I never wanted to take up swimming.

I Can't Breathe

April 30, 2011. I had planned to run the Christie Clinic Marathon in Champaign, Illinois, with two Chicago friends as we attempted to qualify for the Boston Marathon. We needed to pull off 26.2 miles in less than three hours and forty-five minutes, which my training told me was a distinct possibility. But, they were running, and I was sitting in the sunroom of the West County house I'd lived in for about six months, amid the pile of rubble that had become my life.

It was less than a month since the night my world had come crashing down. I was at a major crossroads, but all I could manage was to lie under a blanket on my leather couch, wanting to give up on life.

The irony of the day wasn't lost on me. Outside, the sun shone brightly, pouring in through the wall of windows. The happy sounds of my kids playing in the yard floated in to meet my ears. But under that blanket, I was in a dark place. I couldn't breathe. My lungs were full of unshed tears I'd held in for too long while pretending I was living a life I loved. In reality, I loathed myself and the hypocritical life I was trapped in.

I received a text from my girlfriends, who'd finished our marathon. It said, "We did it! Boston, here we come!" A photo they'd attached showed them after the race, medals around their necks, huge smiles on their faces, toasting each other with their free post-race beers in plastic cups.

I knew they hadn't meant to hurt me, but their celebration felt like a kick in the gut when I was already down. They had no idea of the emotional pain and suffering I was enduring as I hadn't told them about any of it. They didn't intend to add insult to injury, but I couldn't respond to their text with a congratulatory message. I just retreated further into isolation.

I buried myself more deeply under the blanket and wished water would fill my lungs and let me pass silently into the abyss. I'd already stopped eating. I wanted to give up and could see no way out of my situation. I didn't have the energy to kick to the surface. I couldn't get to the air, and quite honestly, I didn't want to.

Lying there in a twilight state, I was haunted by a recurring nightmare: I jump into the pool and come face-to-face with the little girl in the yellow swimsuit. She opens her eyes wide and stares at me. She opens her mouth as bubbles escape and tries to scream, "Help me!" But her cry is muffled by the water filling her mouth and lungs. Then I realize it's not her but it's me.

I'm at the bottom of the pool, staring at my own self. She grabs for me to pull her back to the surface. I can't save both of us. I have to choose. I try to kick my legs, but I'm too paralyzed with fear to do anything. My head throbs, and I hear my mind pleading with me to try. But I'm drowning, and I don't want to save either of us; I'm okay with slipping into the peacefulness of whatever lies beyond.

The happy sound of my children playing outside jarred me back to reality. I had to figure out a way to get back to the surface, to breathe. But how? I was drowning in a sea of depression.

It had begun with my unresolved grief over losing my dad almost a decade earlier. I was pulled in deeper by the loss of my sister-in-law a few months later. Piled on to that was the fact that I'd spent so many years feeling trapped in a marriage that dragged me down. I was filled with self-doubt and had lost my identity. I'd not only compromised myself, I'd also given away my ability to feel, along with any recollection of what it was like to use my voice unmuffled by water.

7: GLIMPSING HOPE

I continued my weekly sessions with my counselor, Jen, and we began to unpack all of the things that had first brought me to her office. I always wore a hat pulled down over my face. My clothes hung on me; the stress had taken its toll on my weight. My issues at the surface were just the beginning. I needed to go deeper.

I was stuck in a state of indecision about my marriage, unsure which path to take, so most of our conversations centered around that. I'd begun to accept that I didn't have to stay trapped like a caged bird, but I still struggled with the overwhelming feeling that I couldn't escape on my own. I didn't believe I possessed the life skills or the ability to be independent. I'd been threatened, manipulated, and controlled into thinking I was worthless, and when someone tells you that often enough, you eventually believe it. I was terrified that my kids would be taken away from me.

After several months of spending at least an hour a week sitting on Jen's couch, I had some new information to unfold into the mix of grief, abuse, depression, and trauma I'd hidden from the world, and from myself, for far too long. I knew this revelation would turn my life on its head even more.

My body felt extra heavy as I climbed the stairs to Jen's second-floor office. I sat down feeling every bit of the weight of what I was going to tell her about my conversation with my husband earlier that day.

"So, a weird thing happened today," I began.

She raised her eyebrows and cocked her head to the side, indicating she was listening. "Yeah?"

"Today something came up in a conversation at home. I'm not sure how to tell this story, so I guess I'll just say it."

Sitting in Jen's office, the story poured out of me as my chin quivered and silent tears began to fall.

I was thirteen, I was in eighth grade, and I liked to dress in matching outfits with my best friend, pretending that we were twins. We listened to Debbie Gibson and Milli Vanilli, singing into our hairbrushes as if they were microphones. My light shone so brightly—until there was an abrupt shift.

He was eighteen, and he was in my youth group at church. We were friends, but we started to like each other more and more. I thought I was pretty special, getting so much attention from someone older. He'd drive over to my house and hang out with me. He even went with my family to our cottage at Spring Lake. I was only rarely allowed to ride in his truck; I had to get special permission. My mom was constantly concerned about his age. But being an adolescent girl, I'd whine, "Oh, Mom, don't worry so much."

I'm not exactly sure how we went from being friends to my becoming his "secret girlfriend," but somewhere along the way, it happened. He said he could see a future with me. We knew no one else could know because of our age difference. We wrote notes and passed them secretly. We held hands when no one was looking. And then we started kissing. We were very careful to not get caught. We were the epitome of a "bad secret."

During the summer months, my bedroom would get hot, so I'd often sleep on the couch in the basement where it was cooler. If there was a breeze, I'd leave the sliding glass door open and just close the screen so I could fall asleep to the sound of the crickets.

One night, my secret boyfriend came in the back door so we could watch TV together. We started kissing. I liked the kissing. I felt his hands through my oversized Garfield nightshirt.

There were other nights when he visited, and we did the same. Then one night, he told me he wanted to "teach" me something. I didn't have a clue what he meant, but I trusted him, so I didn't argue. I sat next to him on the couch with my knees pulled up tight against my chest. His breathy words were hot on my ear, as he placed my little-girl fingers around his male anatomy and said, "You hold it like a baseball bat."

I repeated the words, "I don't want to do this, I don't want to do this, I don't want to do this" over and over. But sadly, I said them only to myself. Those words never came out of my mouth.

I wish I could say that was where it ended.

The rest of that night, and other nights after that, became a blur, their snapshots permanently etched in my brain. Though I was consciously aware in that moment, I didn't understand what was happening. My young mind couldn't grasp it, so it went into shutdown mode. The details were irrelevant; the damage had already been done. My innocence was gone, and that was the beginning of my journey down a path to complete powerlessness. My light had gone dim, and my voice had gone silent.

I still smiled my big Lindsey smile. But behind that smile, there was hurt and confusion, frustration and anger, guilt and shame that no thirteen-year-old should have to endure—that no person of any age should have to endure.

I began to believe I had no say in what anyone did to me. My body had no beginning and no end, no boundaries. I existed for the rest of the world to do with as they saw fit. I saw myself as ugly and unlovable. I wasn't good enough, and I never would be. And yet, I put a smile on my face and carried on.

A few months later, my family moved back to Michigan, which made it easy to shove that ugly, shameful thing down into the deepest part of me. But it was there, permeating my being.

Through most of high school, I adamantly spoke out against sex, to the point that I got teased for being a prude, which was ironic, as it was a complete contrast to the dirty whore I believed myself to be. The very idea of anything sexual elicited fear and shame in me.

After high school, I went to college and earned a bachelor of science degree in family community services. I did volunteer work with low-income, high-risk families. I completed an internship in foster care and adoption, where my cases included children of alcoholics and schizophrenics. I worked as a crisis counselor, and witnessed firsthand the worst that could happen to people, and it broke my heart. I had a heart for helping people who'd been traumatized in the worst ways.

But my own trauma finally came to the forefront. I'd neglected the very part of myself that I'd carefully tended in others. I wanted to go back and tell that little girl it wasn't her fault—that even though she trusted him, let him in the back door, and was too paralyzed with fear to speak up for herself, she didn't do anything wrong.

I wanted to fix other people's problems, because it was easier than taking a look inside to fix myself. I knew that abuse wasn't always outwardly violent. Sometimes it was forced harshly by a stranger, other times by a loved one. But sometimes it was so subtle that it was hardly perceptible. Sometimes, victims almost appeared to cooperate when the abuse came at the hands of someone they trusted, someone they were afraid to hurt or say "no" to. The victims could be groomed to allow it.

When Jen and I peeled the layers back to reveal the root cause of my feelings and emotions, I started to view my life and the choices I now faced in an entirely different light.

Vindication

The night of April 30, after spending the day under a blanket on the couch, I sat at the dinner table across from my husband. I pushed food around my plate, putting nothing into my mouth. The kids were at their cousins' house. It was just the two of us at the table.

He tried to initiate conversation, but I didn't have anything more to say. I slumped down in my chair, and then he said something that caught my attention. He was apologizing to me. At first, I didn't understand what for. He said things that didn't make any sense to me. Finally, I started asking questions. Maybe I just started asking the right questions, or maybe he was now ready to answer them truthfully, without the false pretense of nobility.

As I learned, he wasn't the perfect spouse he'd made himself out to be. He'd been unfaithful, too, on more than one occasion. Our marriage had been a broken mess for much longer than I'd imagined. My head spun.

I thought of all the pain and anguish I'd experienced for the past month—and here he was telling me I wasn't the only one at fault. I felt stunned, confused, and somewhat vindicated. And my heart felt a teeny-tiny flutter of hope. Maybe there was a way out of the hell I'd been living after all.

Revelations at IHOP

It was two weeks later, the middle of May 2011. I felt dizzy, as if I'd just stepped off a carousel that was going way too fast. I had no idea which way was up. Mom had come for a visit to check on me, and after church, we went to IHOP for pancakes. The kids had gone with their dad to his parents' house for their weekly Sunday brunch.

My marriage was in an awkward, uncomfortable phase, and I no longer had the energy to pretend. Rather than fake it with the in-laws, Mom and I did our own thing.

When we finished our meal, we sipped our coffee and talked mostly about how trapped I felt. I was stuck in a house with a husband who was working from home, on a hiatus from travel, as we attempted to repair a relationship that seemed irreparably broken. I took the kids to school, and I picked them up. The hours in between blurred together. I wanted to run, but my body felt weak and shriveled from my lack of eating. If I mustered the energy to run, it was minimal. As my appetite returned, so did my desire to run, but I was nowhere close to full speed. My life was broken, and I felt totally lost and useless.

"You need a job," Mom said, "something to get you out of the house, give you a pursuit of your own. Is there anything around here that'd be an interesting distraction for you?"

I gazed out the window as she asked the question. My eyes fell on a sign above a store across the street.

"Fleet Feet," I said quickly, as if it were the most obvious thing in the entire world. That's where I'd just purchased a new pair of running shoes.

That set a plan in motion. The following week, I went into the Fleet Feet store by the IHOP. As I sifted through a rack of running tops, a sales associate named Bri approached. We talked for a moment and then moved toward the register to pay.

Summoning my courage, I asked, "Do you know if you guys are hiring?"

"Oh, sure!" Bri responded. "Here, let me give you Debbie's business card. She and her husband, David, own the chain of stores in St. Louis, but she handles all the hiring. So send her an email with your resume."

"Thanks!" I said, as she handed me my bag, and we smiled at each other. "Hopefully, I'll see you soon!"

"For sure! Thanks for coming in!"

I floated out of the store, feeling a mix of excitement and terror—but at least I recognized my own emotions again.

I went straight home and dug up an old resume. Eight years had passed since I'd left the workforce. I was embarking on new territory, but I had to keep moving forward.

I updated my resume and wrote a killer cover letter. Even though I didn't have much confidence in myself, I was sure that I could still write well enough to convince them to give me a shot.

Within twenty-four hours, I had an interview lined up to meet with Debbie and Katie, a buyer/manager, at one of the three locations of Fleet Feet stores. I showed up for my meeting a few days later wearing a brand-new pair of gray slacks from the Gap. I'd lost so much weight that nothing else fit—nothing that was appropriate for an interview, anyway.

I walked through the door and was immediately greeted by an associate in a red Fleet Feet shirt with an image of the iconic Saint Louis arch over the lettering. My heart raced as if I'd run a sprint rather than simply walked the fifty feet from the parking lot.

"Hi, I'm Lindsey," I told her. "I'm here to see Debbie."

"I'll let her know you're here," she said, walking toward the back of the store.

I wandered casually and eyed the shoes on display until Debbie arrived and greeted me, sticking out her hand as we introduced ourselves. She led me to the rear of the store and apologized for the mess, explaining they were in the midst of expanding the warehouse and renovating the office space. We walked past her husband, David, who waved as he continued a phone call. Debbie introduced me to Katie, and the three of us sat at a makeshift desk with plastic draped around to hold the dust at bay.

"Rather than ask you typical interview-type questions, we want to get to know you, to see if this might be a good fit for you to come on board," Debbie said as I got settled.

Debbie's approach helped put me at ease. I knew I didn't have any knowledge of sales, but I did have a passion for our mutual hobby. With running the focus, conversation was comfortable and flowed easily. We talked about our favorite marathon stories and what races we were training for, which led naturally into the business part of the interview.

"I know most of my experience is from years ago, before I stayed at home with my kids," I said. "And I haven't worked retail before. But I'm very familiar with customer service from working in membership at AOA."

I explained that my life was going through some adjustments, and I was trying to reestablish my sense of purpose. I didn't go into great detail about what I meant, but I was genuine, and I didn't hide the fact that my life was somewhat messy.

"How do you feel about a retail schedule?" Debbie asked. "We do require one weekend shift and one closing shift per week. I know that can be a strain on family life. If you need to talk it over with your husband, we'd completely understand that."

"Oh, yeah, we're prepared for that. I'm sure it will be fine," I answered out loud, while inwardly thinking that if things at home continued on the current trajectory, I'd need the job regardless of the requirement to work one weekend shift and one closing each week.

"I've always been passionate about running," I told Debbie and Katie. "It'd be great to work in an environment where I can share my enthusiasm for the sport I love."

I told them my sister-in-law had recently passed away unexpectedly and that we were planning a memorial run in California on the one-year anniversary of her death. As I told them the details, they both fought back tears. Based on their sincerity and compassion, the job certainly seemed like a good fit to me.

As we said our goodbyes, and I walked out into the sunshine, I knew I'd found my people.

The next day, I opened my email to find a message from Debbie offering me a position as a part-time sales associate. Getting the job offer was a huge notch up for my self-confidence, which had gradually, over the course of almost eleven years of marriage, plummeted to an epic low. They were willing to take a chance on a stay-at-home mom who loved running. If I accepted, I'd start training on Memorial Day. I was thrilled.

Fleet Feet proved to be exactly what I needed. It got me out of the house, gave me something to focus my energy on, created an instant community for me in a still relatively new environment, and rekindled my desire to do the thing I loved most—run!

Sales didn't come naturally for me right away. I was slow to learn the ins and outs. However, on the flip side, I had a way with customers that drew them in and established credibility. It didn't take long until I considered Fleet Feet more of a home than the house I was living in—or rather, surviving in.

They immediately outfitted me in my new running gear and red shirts. I went through the fit process to learn how to determine the right shoes for other runners or walkers, learning about foot type, gait, and technical gear. There was so much more to the job than just helping a customer pick a pretty color and ringing up the sale at the register, but I was determined, and I kept at it. I could feel my self-confidence building.

8: BREAKING UP

After the disaster of April, as I started to pull myself back together, Jen and I talked about how I could take care of myself. That idea seemed unfathomable; I'd been conditioned to take care of everyone else. But I started to understand the concept of putting on my own oxygen mask first. If I didn't tend to myself, I wouldn't be healthy enough to take care of anyone else.

Besides my new job, I needed a fun goal. I'd started to eat again, which gave me the energy necessary to run. I desperately wanted to get some distance from the tensions at home, and my bosses at Fleet Feet encouraged us to do what we loved. I needed a goal race.

I scoured the marathon calendar to find the right race. In view of the summer heat, I looked for something north. Way north. I discovered that Quebec City offered a full marathon that was a certified Boston qualifier course. Although it took place in August, it offered a more moderate climate and seemed like the adventure I needed.

I requested the time off from work, made airline and hotel reservations, and registered for my race. I was reasonably trained, feeling fortunate to be getting a do-over from the April disappointment.

Setting off to Canada for my first solo international trip, I was more excited than nervous. On check-in at the hotel, I received my choice of upgrades due to my husband's VIP status, and I opted for access to the lounge on the top floor. After dropping my luggage in my room, I decided to check out the view from the lounge.

Guests milled about as they enjoyed a buffet of snacks. Wine and beer were complimentary, but with my goal race a day away, I selected a bottled water. Through the floor-to-ceiling windows,

I took in the stellar views of Quebec City, the river, and the historic fortress.

CNN on the big-screen TV caught my eye. Hurricane Irene was aimed up the east coast, and it looked as if she might track into Canada. I sat down on the couch, sipped my water, and watched the weather report, thinking, "Surely we won't have any effects of this storm here."

As dusk gave way to dark, I went out for a walk through the streets of Quebec City. After wandering through a couple boutiques and grabbing a bite to eat, I turned in at a decently early hour and didn't rise from bed the next morning until I woke up on my own, a luxury for a mom of small children.

After a quick shower and dressing in casual clothes, I sought out a neighborhood coffee shop and purchased a cup to go. There was a garden near my hotel, where I sat to sip my morning beverage. It was a gorgeous, sunny day without a cloud in the perfect, blue sky. With less than twenty-four hours until race day, I hoped for more of the same. But according to the weather forecast, Hurricane Irene was headed right for Quebec City.

I spent the day doing things for myself. I went to the expo to pick up my race packet, laid out my gear for race day, and relaxed with a book. That evening, I enjoyed a lovely dinner at a little Italian place a short walk away.

Before going to sleep, I clicked on the TV to catch the latest weather report. It looked more and more likely that Irene was on her way. I hoped I could get through my forty-two kilometers before things got really nasty. Rain was okay, but I hoped to avoid strong wind.

Race day morning, the jangle of the hotel wakeup call startled me from sleep. I eased out of bed and prepared to catch the shuttle to the start. The Quebec City Marathon was a point-to-point race, meaning the course started in one place and ended in a different location rather than being a giant loop. I'd chosen my hotel based on its proximity to the finish, so I could easily walk back when I was done. In addition, my hotel was exactly where the shuttles were stationed to take us to the start. After confirming a late checkout to allow for a post-race shower before my flight home, I made my way outside.

The sky was misty and gray, but that didn't dampen my mood. I'd worked hard and looked forward to this redemption run with great anticipation. I was confident in my shot at qualifying for the Boston Marathon before they lowered the qualifying times in a few weeks. My nerves only added to my adrenaline.

Yellow school buses lined up in front of the hotel. Paper signs taped to the windows indicated their destination. I noticed several buses going to the start of the half-marathon, which was a different location than the full because it was only half the distance to the same finish.

As I stood on the sidewalk, puzzled, I heard a voice ask, "Do you need help with anything?"

"Yeah, uh, where are the shuttles for the full marathon?"

"There aren't any. That race was canceled. Everyone is running the half."

He continued talking, explaining something about needing to shut down the bridges by a certain time with the expected wind gusts, but I didn't register his words. I'd heard all I needed to. I stood staring at him, slack-jawed and devastated.

Eventually, I dragged myself up the steps of the bus and slumped down into a seat next to a girl who appeared to be near my age. She sensed my obvious disappointment and shared the sentiment. We talked about the rug that had just been yanked out from under us. She, too, had hoped to qualify for Boston, and while it was possible to qualify with a half-marathon time, it had to exceed the pace I was capable of running.

A fellow runner in another seat piped up and tried to keep us positive. "Can't you run a different race next weekend or something?"

Did he think I was made of money and opportunities to go flitting about the world to run marathons? It wasn't that simple.

I shook my head sadly as I wiped away tears. "No. It's not in the cards for me."

This was my only shot. When I got back to Missouri, I would be neck-deep in a messy divorce. Time and funds and sanity would be limited. I was depleted. My motivation was gone. The wind had been stolen from my slack sails—ironic, considering it was the wind that destroyed my race hope.

The shuttles dropped us at the start, and I moved through the motions. I dropped my gear bag so it would be waiting for me at the finish. Then I lined up at the start with all the other runners wearing bibs for both the half and the full marathon. I slurped down a packet of Gu to boost my energy.

The race was uneventful. I tried to take in the scenery, but I really wasn't interested. As the herd moved over the bridge, I held tightly to the visor on my head. Even then, it was challenging not to get blown away by the gusts. Clearly, the officials had made the right call, demoralizing as it was.

As I cruised across the finish line, a volunteer awarded me a medal for the full marathon.

"I didn't run the full," I said, confused.

The volunteer explained, "Oh, right. Well, there aren't enough half-marathon medals for everyone, so anyone wearing a full marathon bib gets a full marathon medal." She offered a half smile.

Having run only 13.1 miles, I didn't want a medal I hadn't earned. I accepted it anyway, as there was no other option.

I waited in line to get my gear as the rain picked up. Goose bumps prickled my skin, and I pulled the mylar wrap I'd been handed at the finish more tightly around my shoulders. The wind blew fiercely, and the rain came down in sheets. I was drenched by the time I got to the front of the line to retrieve my bag. Although I shivered in the cold, I didn't want to waste time putting on clothes that would quickly become soaked, so I began to trod up the hill to the hotel.

I noticed other athletes walking nearby, little lights on their medals blinking. "Okay, so that's kind of cool," I thought to myself. I looked at the medal that hung around my neck and turned it over in my hand. I pulled the little plastic tag out. One blink, another blink, then nothing. I examined it as closely as I could while I walked uphill juggling armfuls of gear and post-race snacks, battling what had turned into hurricane-force winds and rain. The lights on my medal seemed to be broken.

I didn't have it in me to go back to the finish area to exchange it. I no longer cared. It felt appropriate that I had a broken finisher's medal for a race I hadn't run. By the time I got back to the hotel, my face was smeared with a mix of tears and rain. I felt utterly dejected, and I invited myself to a grand pity party. I was pretty sure I was done with running for a while. Or maybe for good.

9: MAKING UP

As summer gave way to fall, working at Fleet Feet convinced me not to break up with running. I needed to refresh our relationship with opportunities that didn't pile on so much pressure.

On a chilly October morning, I met with several of my coworkers at one of the biggest races in town, the Rock-n-Roll Marathon. We weren't there to run but to provide aid for the thousands of runners who'd need support. Before the sun was even close to showing itself, our aid-station crew had gathered. We assembled tables, mixed huge coolers of Gatorade, and poured it into cups organized and stacked on the tables.

The sun started to peek over the buildings, and the Fleet Feet team was ready. At the beginning, we chatted and goofed around until runners finally started coming by. Music blared through a speaker, and our boss, David, spoke into a microphone to greet the runners. We handed out cups of Gatorade as we cheered on runner after runner. I waved at people I knew from working in the store. I had a new appreciation for all the volunteers at my many past races. It was tough work, but I found it so fun that my face hurt from smiling. It was refreshing to be a part of something bigger than myself.

After the pack thinned, we swept up the thousands of paper cups scattered in the street. We still whooped it up for the walkers who came through and then for the folks who brought up the very back of the pack. I was impressed with their determination and unwavering commitment. They struggled, but they weren't willing to call it quits. They kept going, albeit slowly, putting one foot in front of the other, no matter how hard it was.

The sweeper came through, indicating there were no more runners. We finished cleaning up, loaded our gear back onto the trucks, and made our way back to our cars.

Having worked the expo and some additional shifts earlier that week, I didn't have to hurry to work at the store that day. Despite having gotten out of bed at three in the morning, I overflowed with energy, so I headed to Creve Coeur Lake for a run, glad that I always kept spare gear in my car.

A considerable number of the area runners had participated in the Rock-n-Roll events, so I pulled into a mostly empty parking lot. It was a nice day to be outside but still chilly. I did a quick change and laced up my Mizunos, hoping to run thirteen miles, a half-marathon in honor of the runners I'd just witnessed.

I started my Garmin and set out around the lake. I completed one loop and felt great. After another loop, I still had more in the tank. At the end of my third loop, I'd run just over fifteen miles. I couldn't stop without rounding it out, so I topped it off to finish at sixteen miles. It was still there. I still loved running.

I hopped back in my car, feeling exhausted and satisfied. I knew I had another marathon in me. When and where were the questions I had to figure out. I was confident that the how would work itself out.

Dallas with Dad

After I got home and showered, I sat down at my computer and started looking for another race. I needed at least six weeks to get myself ready again after the Great Canadian Running Boycott. Looking at the options, I found the perfect race almost instantly. It was obvious.

The Dallas Whiterock Marathon would take place on December 4, 2011. My dad had run Dallas Whiterock thirty years earlier, and it was scheduled for the weekend marking the tenth anniversary of his death. I wanted to do it for him. I needed to do it for me. So, I set the wheels in motion to try again.

To appease my husband, I promised to keep my race expenses low. I bought a cheap airline ticket and made a reservation at a hotel that turned out to be somewhat sketchy.

After my plane landed in Dallas, I took the bus from the airport into downtown Dallas. When I stepped onto the bus, the bus driver took one look at me and said, "Sit right here where I can see you. And don't take your hand off your suitcase." What had I done to make the driver act so peculiarly?

As we waited for the bus to fill, he asked what had brought me to Dallas, and I told him about my marathon and my dad. "I know your dad is with you and that he's very proud of you," the driver said. To pass the time, I pulled out a book and tried to read. As the bus bounced along, I casually looked up and noticed the guy across from me peering over the top of his 80s-style shades, the kind with slats like shutters. I tried to return to my book quickly, but it was too late.

"Are you a student?" he asked.

"No," I answered, puzzled.

"Because you look really smart," he said awkwardly.

"Oh, Lord, help me!" I thought to myself.

"You leave her alone!" the bus driver snapped at him.

I shot the driver a relieved smile in his rearview mirror and kept my eyes on my book until we reached the end of the route.

Ideally, I would have gotten off within walking distance of my hotel, but I had to transfer to another bus to reach the hotel. The driver told me to wait on the bus and he'd show me where to go. After all the other passengers had disembarked, he walked me to the spot where I needed to wait.

Having lived for many years in Chicago, I was comfortable taking public transportation. I wondered if I was giving off a damsel-in-distress vibe or if the driver just needed to be protective. Regardless, I was grateful for his help, and I told him so.

After another short bus ride and a two-block walk, I arrived at my hotel and got settled. I walked around the corner and across the street to the beautiful race headquarter hotel where fresh cookies were being served in the lobby.

"Excuse me, where are the shuttles to the marathon expo?" I asked a hotel employee.

"They're out the side doors," she informed me.

"Thanks," I said, regretting my decision not to stay at the headquarters hotel.

Several charter buses sat in the circle drive. I jumped on one of them, and it delivered me to the convention center for the Health and Fitness Expo. I picked up my race packet, wandered around for a while, and then grabbed a seat on the shuttle back to the downtown area. I wasn't at all excited about going back to my less-than-superb accommodations.

I sat staring out the window when I heard a woman with a charming Southern drawl ask if she could sit next to me. Enter Judy.

Judy and I talked as we traveled back to headquarters. She told me about all of the marathons and other major races she'd completed. I could count mine on two hands; Judy had many more to her credit. A mom, grandma, and nurse, Judy had done an IRONMAN. I was duly impressed. To top it all off, she was one of the sweetest people I'd ever met. I told her I was going through a divorce and learning to be a single mom and that I worked at Fleet Feet.

Judy told me about triathlons and IRONMAN; I informed her I was a runner and nothing more. My friend Lindsey Farrell was training for an IRONMAN.

"I'm never doing an IRONMAN," I declared matter-of-factly.

"Never say never," she said knowingly. "You might surprise yourself someday, when you learn how capable you are. Yeah, you'll do one," she nodded. "You might even become a nurse."

I laughed. As nice as this stranger was, she had no clue. I told her that I'd once thought I might do something medical, but that was before my dad died. I didn't have room in my life for IRONMAN triathlons and school and all this craziness she was talking about. No way.

We discussed our race plans for the following day. The weather forecast looked dismal. I'd put too much pressure on myself in Quebec, and I didn't want to do that again.

"I'm just planning to go for a run through Dallas with my dad's spirit guiding the way."

"Sometimes that's the best race plan there is," she smiled.

By the time we arrived back at Judy's hotel room, we'd enjoyed getting to know each other, so we swapped phone numbers. We both planned to eat at the pre-race pasta dinner that evening and agreed to look for each other there.

I went to my hotel to drop off my packet and relax for a bit. I watched an episode of *Friends* on TV and kept one eye open for cockroaches; then I grabbed my umbrella and walked back to dinner in the big conference hall. I fixed myself a plate of salad, bread, and pasta and looked around for a nearby table with a few empty seats. I planned to text Judy after I sat down.

As I set my plate on the table and looked to my right, there was Judy. What were the odds that in the huge room full of people that I would sit down next to the only person I knew?

We picked up our earlier conversation, discussing race day details. I wasn't entirely sure what I was going to do, since I had to check out of my hotel before I finished running. I guessed I'd leave my suitcase with the front desk and clean up in the lobby restroom as best I could before flying back to Missouri. Judy insisted that I drop off my stuff to her room in the morning, and she'd give me an extra key so I could shower there, as I was likely to finish before her.

I couldn't believe my luck. Who was this woman who was restoring my faith in humanity by being so encouraging and generous to me? Me, a perfect stranger. But we agreed that you meet people for a reason. Little did I know that this stranger from the South, who lived in Boston, would continue to be a part of my story.

The next morning, I checked out of my room and wheeled my suitcase to Judy's room across the street. Then we headed to the race course amidst a herd of people wrapped in trash bags, trying to protect themselves from the dampness of the fog and rain that was settling in. Facing a high temp of low forties and a fairly brutal wind, I went into the race knowing it wasn't about a Boston qualifying time or even a personal best. I just wanted to run the best race I could and remember my dad.

We slopped through puddles as we ran, and my shoes were soaked within the first mile. Around mile four, the clouds opened up in a total downpour, but I smiled as I tilted my head to the sky and felt the rain on my face.

We faced wind, rain, sleet, and cold for 26.2 miles. At mile twenty, I tried to open my belt containing personal items to retrieve some Sports Beans, jelly beans with extra electrolytes, but my fingers were frozen despite the gloves I wore.

A volunteer at the water station helped me out and sent me on my way for the last six miles, a slight downhill into the finish. I ran my heart out in the most miserable conditions imaginable, carrying the spirit of my dad with me. I felt him there, pushing me along, encouraging me, giving me my reason to smile every cold step of the way.

When I finally crossed the finish and blew a kiss to the sky, I beamed as I looked at the clock. My time didn't qualify me for Boston, but I'd run a new personal best. At officially three hours and forty-seven minutes, it was the best run of my life—a run for my dad. Tears of pride and joy mingled with the rain drops on my face.

I pulled the key to Judy's room from the zippered pocket of my running tights, turned on the hot water of the shower, and let the steam warm me before I stepped in. I quickly got ready to go to the airport, but, still basking in my race joy, I didn't bother with public transportation. Instead, I had the bellman hail a cab. I regretted not finding out how Judy had done, but I knew I'd see her again someday. I just had no idea where that would be.

10: FINDING COURAGE

In the world of triathlon, as in running, there are different categories. The shortest triathlons are called sprints, reasonably enough. A sprint-distance tri consists of a short swim, a 12-mile bike ride, and a 5k to finish. An Olympic-distance triathlon is approximately double that. From there, it steps up to a half distance IRONMAN, which is obviously half the distance of a full distance IRONMAN. An full distance IRONMAN triathlon is a 2.4-mile swim, a 112-mile bike, and a 26.2-mile run, all totaling 140.6 miles.

Marathons and IRONMAN races are special in that they allow the opportunity for average amateur age-group athletes to compete on the same platform as professionals. At any race, there are all levels of abilities. There are average athletes, there are elites, and then there are people like Teri Griege.

I'll never forget the first time I met Teri. It was a Monday evening, and I'd been on staff at Fleet Feet only a few months when she came in looking for gear with her daughter, Kati.

Several of us were working that night. Still in training, I was like a puppy on Faith's heels, following her everywhere and trying to soak up her natural charisma on the sales floor. She showed Teri one thing after another; Teri took in Faith's advice.

"So, what is it that you're needing this for?" Faith asked her.

"I was invited to be an inspirational athlete at the IRONMAN World Championship in Kona, Hawaii, this fall, and they're sending a crew to interview me this weekend," she answered.

We stood there, slack-jawed and wide-eyed, staring at Teri for half a second before Faith started firing questions at her, while intermittently showing her something else she needed.

There are triathlons, and then there are IRONMAN triathlons. And then there is THE triathlon—the IRONMAN World Championship held in Kona, Hawaii, for the best athletes in the world.

Teri proceeded to tell us her story. In 2009, she had attempted to qualify for the IRONMAN World Championship by placing in her age group at IRONMAN Louisville.

"I'd trained hard, but it wasn't as smooth as the previous year. I'd dealt with injuries and fatigue, and, while my ultimate goal was to qualify for Kona, on race day, I didn't feel like myself. It was more of a struggle than normal. I thought I had overtrained."

We were captivated.

"I was crushed that I missed my goal of qualifying by only a few minutes, but the real tragedy came two weeks later when my family made me go to the doctor. I was diagnosed with Stage IV colon cancer, which has a poor prognosis. I had surgery to remove the tumors, and we fought the cancer with chemo. Through everything, I kept on training."

I looked around at my coworkers and saw I wasn't the only one with tears in my eyes.

"It was still my dream to get to Kona. I raced at IRONMAN Florida last year with the same goal. I didn't want to miss any opportunity, even while undergoing treatment, so I sent off an email to a producer at NBC. I figured I didn't have anything to lose."

She heard back from him almost immediately, but he needed a couple weeks to give her an official answer. A few days before her fiftieth birthday, she got it. Teri was going to Kona. And she was taking cancer with her.

By the time she finished telling her story, those of us standing by the counter listening to her were awestruck. Some of us wiped tears away; we couldn't really find words. No one could believe the determination, the sheer heart, and pure grit of the inspirational woman who stood before us. Her positive attitude and perseverance in the face of a frightening, life-threatening medical condition made her glow like an angel.

Faith asked for Teri's phone number so our coworker, Amy, could write a story about her for the Fleet Feet newsletter. She graciously and humbly agreed, and we all promised to watch when the story of Kona aired a couple months later.

As inspired as I was by Teri, I had no idea that this accidental introduction to an angel was, in fact, not an accident at all. I had even less of an idea how she would eventually walk with me on my own IRONMAN journey when triathlon still wasn't even a passing thought in my mind.

11: TAKING BIG STEPS

The morning I filed for divorce, I arrived at work later and was met by my coworker, Lindsey Farrell. We'd quickly become good friends, and since we had the same first name, I'd taken to calling her "Farrell."

I came on the sales floor as Farrell was finishing up with a customer. "Thanks for coming in!" she said, handing him his purchase.

She finished up at the counter, and I went to the computer next to her to clock in. I glanced around to make sure there weren't any other customers in the store before launching into the news I had to tell her.

"Oh my God, Farrell! I'm totally flipping out! You won't believe what I did today!"

"You signed up for an IRONMAN?" she joked, knowing full well I was dead set against swimming.

"I filed for divorce!"

She stopped what she was doing and turned to face me.

"What?" she exclaimed, grabbing me by the shoulders so she could look me straight in the eye. "You did it? Seriously?"

"Yes, I did it," I answered and gave her all the details of the night before: my husband coming home in the middle of the night and how scared I was that he might follow me to the attorney's office.

"Oh my gosh! That's so crazy!" she said. "I'm proud of you! You're so brave."

"I don't feel brave," I said. "I feel scared to death. I don't know what I'm doing. He's going to flip out."

"He doesn't know yet?"

"No, I'm waiting until we have a session with our counselor to tell him. I honestly don't know what he'll do, and I don't want to be alone with him when he finds out."

"I don't blame you there," she said. "So do you finally get to move out? Or will he?"

"No," I said with defeat. "My attorney wants me to stay until we get things sorted out, and I'm sure he won't willingly go anywhere."

"That's going to suck. But, well, take a deep breath. You're going to be okay. In fact, you're going to be so much better than okay."

I let Farrell's words sink in. She was a calming presence as I came to grips with the fact that I'd taken the first official step to leave a toxic relationship. She had confidence that I'd done the right thing and that things were going to work out, even if I still questioned it.

I relied again on my coworker's support and judgment when, several months later, Farrell and I started talking about the possibility of my training for a triathlon. I was really never one to make New Year's resolutions, but with all the changes going on in my life, it seemed like a good time to try some other new challenges. For me as a runner, it had gotten really easy to just strap on my shoes and go out the door to get some miles. It seemed appropriate in my difficult personal circumstances to pursue some physical challenges as well.

"But I don't swim," I told Farrell. "I mean, I really don't swim. I took a lifeguard certification class in high school, but treading water for a minute while holding a brick over my head didn't exactly help me learn stroke technique."

"I'll help you," she insisted. "Besides, you need a new goal." Because she had held my hand before, I knew I could trust her to do it again.

"Okay," I finally agreed.

First, I researched which race could be my starting point. I proposed the idea of the Chicago Triathlon because it was on familiar ground. It centered around Oak Street Beach, where I'd occasionally jumped in the water to cool off after hot training runs for the 2001 Chicago Marathon. Farrell thought that sounded too demanding and suggested the local Lake Saint Louis Triathlon, which offered the option of both sprint and Olympic distances. In addition, she'd be there to show me the ropes.

I got online and investigated the Lake Saint Louis tri. Even though I couldn't swim and didn't have a bike, I decided to give it a go. And because I never started out small with anything, I went straight for the Olympic distance. It was only a 10k run. Pshhh—I could do that backwards in my sleep. However, I'd never tried to run after being in the water for a mile and then biking a hilly twenty-five miles. Nonetheless, I was sure that part would be fine. I just had to figure out the swim and how to put it all together.

I discovered that attacking my fear of swimming took a little focus off some of my other fears, like my fear of being a single mom and all that would entail. I was terrified of buying a house, securing a mortgage, paying the bills, doing the home and yard maintenance, organizing my finances, keeping the kids alive, paying taxes, maintaining my vehicle, and all the other stuff I didn't even know that I didn't know yet. It was overwhelming. To tackle a tangible fear like swimming helped me realize I could learn new skills. I wasn't perfect at it, but I could do it, which relieved some pressure from the other areas of the unknown.

It was around that same time that I took on the role of Thursday night social run leader at the Chesterfield store. On Thursday evenings, a group of runners would meet at the store and go for a three, four, or five-mile run on a paved trail behind the store. I sent out a weekly email to invite participants, welcomed runners into the store, and kicked off the run. Upon returning to the store, I offered beverages and an occasional treat before heading across the street to a local pizza place with the group.

Steve and I became friends after his first couple of times attending the social run. I told him, "Hey, I signed up for this triathlon at Lake Saint Louis in September. You should do it."

He politely declined, saying, "Yeah, I don't think so." But at the social run the following week, he was proud to announce that, due to his weakness in the face of peer pressure, he'd signed up, too. We were both new to the idea of triathlons, and we were in it together.

A couple months later on a Sunday evening after closing up the store, I went home, popped a frozen pizza in the oven, and pulled up the live feed for the IRONMAN Arizona finish line on my laptop. I was stalking the finishers with eager anticipation, looking for Farrell to come into view. I'd received updates all day from her husband, Ryan, and her mom, Wendy.

I looked at the bracelet around my wrist. When Farrell had signed up for the IRONMAN, I'd bought both of us matching bracelets, leather straps that snapped in place. Each bracelet bore a single word. The one I gave Farrell read "Believe," a gift to remind her she could do exactly what she was attempting to do. Mine read "Courage," because I needed the reminder to stay strong in the face of things that scared me.

I texted our mutual friend Nicole. We were so excited, and we knew it wouldn't be long before Farrell made her dream a reality. She'd trained hard for this, and no one doubted her abilities. As I watched her cross the finish line, I had goosebumps. She'd proven to me that the word *impossible* was only a word.

"This makes me want to do one, too!" Nicole texted.

Not me. I was still content being a spectator in the world of IRONMAN.

I Don't Own a Bike

I'd signed up for a triathlon; that was the first step. There was only one problem: I still didn't own a bike.

Fortunately, not too long thereafter, I was at work one day, helping a customer named Joe with some running shoes. We were discussing what he did for a living, and he explained, "Well, what you do with running shoes, I do with bikes." His timing was perfect, and I promised I wouldn't wait long to pay him a visit at his bike shop in nearby Washington, Missouri.

My mom came to town again a few weeks later to support me and help with my kids as the legal divorce proceedings heated up. Attorney meetings and depositions were really emotionally draining activities woven into my new daily routine. It was especially tough to juggle work, kids, and a volatile divorce when I had few friends and no family nearby, so Mom made a habit of visiting frequently to check in on me.

While she was in town, I mentioned that I wanted to check out a shop to see if they had a bike for me. We took a drive out to see Joe. When we walked in the store, I reminded him how we'd met by asking how he liked his new running shoes. I explained I was ready to check out a bike and asked if he had anything that might work for me on the cheaper end of the spectrum. Since I didn't really know where I was headed with this tri thing, I didn't want to go into more debt than I was already accumulating with attorney's fees for a sport I might try once and then give up forever.

Joe had a blue Trek road bike that fit my needs—pretty basic, but it would serve my purpose fine. If I decided to pursue the sport beyond one race, I could add some upgrades.

Joe brought it out to the sales floor, and I noticed how much it resembled the first bike I'd been given: a light blue ten-speed, for my tenth birthday.

I rode it around in circles through the parking lot. It was a smooth enough ride, and I thought it would get the job done. Joe seemed to think it was a good choice for me.

When it came time to pay, Mom gifted me the money to buy "Little Blue." Joe added a water bottle cage to its frame and threw in a water bottle at no charge. I didn't have a bike rack, so we loaded it in the back of my Pathfinder and away we went.

Now that I had a bike, I was out of excuses.

12: FACING THE TRUTH

As soon as I started running marathons, I became convinced that my determination gave me the strength to run any course I undertook. From 5ks to 50ks, I could go the distance, as long as I knew where the finish line was.

As for my divorce, however, I wasn't prepared for the ever-moving finish line—the uncertainty of knowing when it would be over. How long would I have to suffer through court appearances and live under the same roof as someone who held so much animosity toward me?

It was mentally exhausting and emotionally painful, but somehow it felt better to combat it by abusing myself with running, boxing, yoga, and any other form of physical activity. There was something to be said for endorphins, and they seemed to keep me going through the mental and emotional turmoil of the next several months.

The divorce process was lengthy and cumbersome. My legal team would propose a settlement offer, and then we'd wait. We'd receive a counteroffer and then begin discussions of our own counter. It was a back-and-forth process, with considerable waiting in between. When we couldn't come to an agreement by the fast-approaching trial date, we prepared to present our case to a judge in court.

One day, I sat in a room listening to my attorney interrogate my husband. There were questions about finances and personal issues, but one line of questioning stood out.

"Did you ever have any complaints about Lindsey as a wife and a mother?" my attorney asked.

"Yes."

"Can you elaborate?"

I braced myself for his answer.

"She was selfish and lazy."

"Can you provide some examples? Like, how was she lazy?"

I held my breath, waiting to hear what I'd done to deserve the worst labels I could imagine, labels I'd fought with every ounce of my being not to be.

"Sometimes she takes naps on Sundays."

"Okay, and how is she selfish?"

"Well, she goes to the gym every day, and she's allowed to drop the kids off at childcare for two hours. She uses the full two hours."

"And what does she do during those two hours?"

"She does a workout for the first hour, then takes a shower. Then she'll sit in the café for the second hour, to read or finish her Bible study or whatever."

"Okay, I see," my attorney responded.

I looked around the room, trying to read the faces of everyone else who had listened to his answers. We sat waiting silently to hear if there was more. There wasn't. Were they all as embarrassed as I was at how ridiculous his complaints sounded?

Had I been a perfect wife and mother? No, such a creature never existed. But I'd done my best, and I finally heard the absurdity of his words.

At last, I recognized how much control he'd exerted over what I believed myself to be. I'd spent years fighting to disprove those awful things about myself because I'd been brainwashed to believe them. I'd worked tirelessly to raise three small children, keep a household running, do endless hours of volunteer work, and get up before the sun to run twenty miles to train for a marathon. I'd put everyone before myself to the point of sheer exhaustion.

The idea that I was selfish, stupid, or lazy hung limply in the air until I exhaled and blew those beliefs to pieces.

It finally clicked. The power his words had held over me for so long vanished in that moment. I was done pretending, and his words no longer had the same effect on me.

A week later, it was my turn to answer the questions. The day I gave my deposition was perhaps the most trying day of my entire life. For several hours, I sat in a conference room with my attorney next to me and my almost-former spouse and his attorney across the table. To my right, the court reporter tapped out everything I said. More specifically, she tapped out my answers to the questions posed with the purpose of making me appear unstable and unfit to raise my children.

These questions probed everything I'd ever done wrong during my years as a wife and a mother, exposing every secret I had. I cried occasionally; my attorney requested a brief recess so I could go outside for a breath of air. My attorney came with me, and we sat on the curb.

"You're doing great. It's okay to get emotional. These are hard questions and difficult topics. Being vulnerable shows the court you're a human being."

"I want to scream," I said.

"Well, now's your chance." He was giving me permission.

I looked at him, and he shrugged, "Why not?"

So, I did. I let out a gut-wrenching wail.

"Feel better?" he asked.

"Kinda," I nodded slightly. Then I laughed.

"Okay, are you ready to finish this up?"

"I guess so," I said, rising to my feet and brushing the dirt from my dress.

I took a deep breath as my attorney opened the door for me, pulled myself together, and went back inside for another round of questioning.

Under oath, I admitted to my faults and failures, to every mistake I'd ever made. I shared the worst parts about myself and told the truth, the whole truth, and nothing but the truth. As painful as it was, it left me feeling a huge sense of relief. I was stronger than I'd ever felt in my life.

When I faced myself in a mirror of honesty, the reflection showed how broken I was. But I also saw that I was on the road to restoration. I saw that all the awful things I'd come to believe about myself over the course of eleven years of marriage weren't true.

I'd messed up from time to time, and some of those mess-ups were big ones. But I owned my mistakes. I was human, and when it came down to it, I was a good mom with a big heart. Anyone could see I was willing to work hard to fix the broken parts of myself, to be the best I could for my children.

I walked out of that office into the spring sunshine and held my tear-streaked face high. As difficult as the experience had been, I'd made it. I felt exhausted, relieved, and alive. I'd done what I needed to do, and I'd done it well. And if I had to get on the stand in court and do it again, I knew I could.

A month or so later, trial day was upon us. My attorney had grilled and prepped me, and I arrived ready to be strong. However, that proved to be a lot of fanfare for little reason. The judge pulled counsel from both sides into her chambers and told them there was no reason to take the case to trial. She didn't care what I'd done wrong in the past; she wanted us to come to a settlement that was best for the kids.

We went back and forth a few times until we came to an agreement. The judge was on board. We still had to file it with the court and wait for the seal of approval, which could take another month or two. We were a step closer. So close and yet so far away.

My husband and I started following the custody schedule even though I didn't yet have the means to buy a house of my own. It was better for everyone that we didn't all live under the same roof, the roof that sometimes felt as if it might blow off from all the tension inside. We took turns living at the marital house based on who had custody of the kids. When I was there, he traveled for work or stayed with his parents. When he was there, I stayed with my friend Katrina, who was also newly single and had a spare room.

Katrina and I worked together at Fleet Feet, and several of our shifts overlapped. We also enjoyed getting together on our shared days off. We'd cook meals together, watch TV, and play the song, "Just Dance." On Sundays after work, we'd hit downtown St. Charles for dinner and drinks on Main Street. Even though Katrina's divorce didn't involve children, we were both learning to navigate some hard things, and we appreciated each other's support.

The first day of the new school year for my kids snuck up on me, as it fell on a day they were with their dad. When it dawned on me that for the first time ever, I wasn't going to be there to pack their lunches, get them into their uniforms, take pictures of them with their new backpacks, and drop them off at school, I was crushed. It was the first of what I knew was only the beginning of a long string of events I would miss with my kids.

I went to Kat's bedroom and knocked on the door.

"Yeah, come in" she said.

I opened the door to find her still in bed, looking at her phone. She immediately saw my tears and stretched out her arms as an invitation. I lay down next to her, and she wrapped her arms around me while I sobbed. She let me cry as long as I needed to and then helped me come up with a plan to modify the first day of school so I could at least get a picture of my kiddos. And eventually she had me laughing.

Living with Kat was helpful on several levels. She'd completed some tough triathlons and was encouraging in that area as well. I often started the day with a run or a bike ride out her front door.

It seemed appropriate that it was the same week as my first triathlon, when I was leaving Kat's house and driving over the river one morning, that I got a call from my paralegal. It was official: The judge had signed the papers, and I was no longer a married woman. I added single mom, divorcee, and triathlete to my titles within a single week. A few days later, I also added homeowner to the list.

I'd reached an invisible, ever-moving finish line, but I was learning it was likely only the first of many to come.

13: TESTING THE WATERS

In a summer full of legal battles and learning to navigate a maze of unknowns, the Lake Saint Louis Triathlon snuck up on me. Before I knew it, race day was right around the corner, and I was considerably less than prepared.

When I'd registered in February, August seemed eons away, so I fell comfortably into the mode of "I've got plenty of time." With a few weeks to go, I'd been in the water to practice the swim sporadically at best. I created excuses, but the truth was that I'd avoided swimming. Open-water swimming was not happening.

Steve checked in with me periodically to ask, "How's the swimming going?"

I often responded by changing the subject.

With the race only a week away, Steve convinced me to join him at Lake Saint Louis for the practice swim. The course was set up and ready to go. All I had to do was pay the fee, and I could practice to my heart's content.

We waded into the water from the beach, and he set off in front of me. I sputtered and spat all the way through the course. Steve did a loop and then caught up to me on his second time around. We side-stroked so we could talk.

"How long do you want to do this?" he grinned.

I retorted, "Can we be done now?"

"Sure. You have to get back to the beach first. Still want to bike?"

"Anything is better than this."

"All right. I'll see you at the beach." Then he zipped away again, looking like Flipper.

I watched him go, sighed heavily, and continued making my way around the orange inflatable buoys.

Steve was waiting on the sand when I finally finished.

"Well, that was horrible," I groaned.

"Let's go ride!" he said enthusiastically.

I glared at him. He grinned at me, which made me break into a smile of my own.

We changed out of our wet clothes, got the bikes ready, and rode through part of the course. It took my legs a while to get going after coming out of the water. I understood why triathletes debated using the kick in the swim or saving their legs for later.

On our way to the parking lot, we pedaled up the last long hill. I shifted gears too late, and my chain started grinding.

"Uh-oh, I think my chain came off!" I yelled.

He circled back around and came up beside me to help. At the exact moment he stopped and put his foot on the ground, my gears clicked in and I was good to go.

"Oh, never mind. I'm good," I said as I took off up the hill, increasing my speed.

He stood staring at me, realizing he had to ride up the hill from a dead stop. "Jerk!" he called after me.

I hadn't meant to leave him in the dust, but we had a good laugh about it when we were back at our cars and I could breathe again.

The morning of the race, I met Nick at Fleet Feet so we could drive to the race together. I'd gotten tired of hauling my bike in the back of my Pathfinder, so I'd caved and bought a bike rack that could transport two bikes. We added his bike to mine and drove toward the race.

We found street parking a couple blocks from the course and dragged our gear over to set up. I rested a crate full of my supplies on the handlebars of my bike as I pushed it down the street. I was wobbly; I hadn't thought to practice that skill.

It was still dark when we arrived at the course. The time had arrived to put it all together: the swim, bike, and run. But first, I had to stage the event and learn how to arrange my transition area.

When we got to the transition area, it was lined with makeshift bike racks. There were lots of athletes already setting up, and we located the racks assigned to us based on our divisions.

I set down the crate, rested my bike against my leg, and pulled out my phone to text Farrell.

She spotted me and took me to a space that could accommodate my bike. I lifted it into the racks, and Farrell started laying out her gear next to her bike. First, she laid down a towel to claim her space. I followed suit. Then she grouped her cycling stuff together: helmet, shoes, socks, race belt with number attached, sunglasses, and nutrition items. Again, I did what she did. Then she put her running gear together. For her, that included a change of shoes, since she had fancy clip-in bike shoes. I had regular bike pedals, so I put on my running shoes for the ride.

"Don't forget to take your helmet off before you go out for the run," she said. "People have done that and had to hold it or wear it the whole run."

I chuckled nervously but set out my visor so I'd remember to swap.

The last items were our swim caps and goggles, which we'd need for the first part of the race. With all our gear set up, it was time to wait for the start.

I was dressed in an old tri kit of Farrell's to represent Fleet Feet. Triathletes wear "kits," multipurpose garments made for quicker transitions and comfort through all three phases of the race. They're sleek in the water, dry quickly, and have a little padding in the crotch for the time spent on the bike.

I attached my timing chip securely around my ankle so it would activate when the race started and track my progress, and Farrell and I took pictures together to commemorate the day. Looking around the transition area, I recognized several familiar faces, including my boss, David. He lived in the Lake Saint Louis community but had never participated in the event. I found it hilarious that he was doing his first-ever triathlon the same day I was.

The athletes congregated on the beach. Farrell and I had found Steve and Nick, and we waited with fellow Fleet Feeters, Katie and her husband, Brian. They'd both completed numerous triathlons, including an IRONMAN. Instead of intimidating me, they encouraged me to complete the race.

Announcements boomed over the loudspeaker, and the national anthem was played. One by one, our group shrank as waves of athletes grouped together by age and gender headed off into the water.

The minutes flew by at lightning speed as my turn rapidly approached. Farrell's group went. Steve's group went.

At the time I signed up, the Olympic distance had seemed like a great idea. As I stood on the sand watching athletes take off, I wondered what I'd gotten myself into. Sure, I could run a 10k with no trouble, but I'd never tackled all three disciplines one right after the other.

Another major issue was that I'd had great intentions of learning to swim well, but life had gotten in the way. So had my fear. I hadn't wanted to risk coming face-to-face with the girl on the bottom of the pool, so I'd come up with every excuse not to swim: It was too cold, I didn't like my wetsuit, I didn't have time, I'd just washed my hair. What it really boiled down to was, I didn't want to know what was lurking in the depths below, waiting to drag me down.

When it came right down to it, I was afraid of putting my face in the water. I didn't want to look down at the bottom, whether I could see it or not. I wanted to make sure I had easy access to oxygen. As my race day had closed in on me, I hadn't gotten any more comfortable in the water.

None of it made sense. I grew up going to Lake Michigan every summer of my life. I loved splashing around in the waves, floating on rafts, and doing handstands in the water, but swimming for distance was not on the agenda. In high school, I completed a lifeguard training course for a PE credit my sophomore year, which included a successful rescue. Mr. Jewell, one of the larger coaches, would coat himself in Vaseline and flail excessively. He made the rescue as difficult as possible for a slender fifteen-year-old girl who weighed around 125 pounds. Somehow, I'd succeeded in my rescue attempt, passed the class, and gained my certification, though I used it only one summer a few years later as a substitute lifeguard for special events.

Standing on the beach, I was not sure how I was going to conquer an almost mile-long swim. Essentially, I was throwing a Hail Mary pass and hoping for the best.

I waded into the water with the other twenty or so athletes in my age group, tugged at my pink swim cap, and adjusted my goggles. The air horn blew, and everyone ran for deeper water. I dove in and swam about ten strokes. I immediately knew I couldn't swim freestyle the entire way. I turned on my side and tried desperately to catch my breath, watching all the pink swim caps that had started with me slip farther and farther into the distance. I'd made up my mind that I couldn't do it before I'd even tried.

Soon, the green swim caps of the men who had started in the wave after mine surrounded me. I worried about getting pushed under. But then, just as quickly as they appeared, they all passed me and were gone. The same thing happened a few more times until all the age groups were in the water. Then most of them were out of the water. Finally, only a few of us remained to finish the swim leg.

As I struggled through the water, something occurred to me. It didn't matter how I got there, but I knew it was important that I make it to dry land. Failure would not be my lame attempt at swimming. Failure was giving up entirely.

I swam around the last buoy and headed for the beach, which still seemed light years away. I kept checking to see if I could touch the bottom. At last, if I pointed my toes, I could feel sand grazing their very tips. I had to keep swimming a little farther. Finally, I was able to put my feet down, and I stumbled through the water and made my way to the sand. I'd completed the swim.

It was awful. It was long and grueling and not fun at all. My performance had not even remotely resembled swimming. But I hadn't drowned. I'd finished the first swim of my triathlon career. It was ugly, but it was a step.

If I was going to do it again, I had to find a swim instructor. In that moment, though, I was unconvinced there would ever be a next time. Next time didn't matter though; I still had work to do.

I pulled my goggles off and felt the swollen rings around my eyes. From the beach, I wobbled up the sidewalk, past the sea of enthusiastic spectators. As unimpressive as my swim had been, I had completed it.

I tried to be quick in the transition to the bike, but I felt encumbered by the wet tri kit I wasn't used to wearing. After minutes that seemed like hours, I snapped my bike helmet into place and pulled my bike from the rack. I awkwardly jogged it to the bike mount line in the street, hopped on, and took off.

I rode through the neighborhood and out to the main road. The bike course was twenty-five miles of rolling hills. I hadn't spent a lot of time training for the bike leg, but it was far better than the swim. My strong runner legs allowed me to fake my way through cycling, and the downhills gave me the chance to coast and recuperate a bit. Strangely, I learned that climbing hills was my strength. I could easily pass bigger, stronger athletes on the way up, but then they'd fly past my tiny body on my not-so-aerodynamic "Little Blue" on the way down.

Nearing the turn back into the neighborhood, I thought I recognized David on the hill in front of me. I pedaled hard and glanced to my right as I passed him.

"Hey, having fun?" I grinned.

"Remind me to never do this again," he said.

I laughed and kept going. I knew he would likely pass me on the run.

As I climbed the last hill into the transition area, several familiar faces called out my name. Even though I was breathing heavily, I gave a slight nod of acknowledgment.

At the top of the hill, I dismounted and returned my bike to the rack. The second transition, or T2 in tri lingo, was much quicker than the first, T1.

After swapping bike helmet for visor and making a couple other small adjustments, I was out of transition and ready for the run. I bolted out on the run course, excited to have made it to the part I enjoyed. Glancing at my Garmin, I saw that my speed was much faster than I could maintain, so I settled into a more reasonable pace. The sun was high in the sky and it was already uncomfortably warm. I knew the temps were going to edge up to dangerous levels.

Within the first half mile of the run, David went flying past me. Even with his Achilles tendon nagging him, it took him less time to catch me than I'd predicted. "At least I had my brief moment of beating my boss," I thought.

The run was hard. It was hilly and hot. The direct sunlight beat down on us, as the course offered almost no shade. Aid stations were a welcome relief, offering cold water and Gatorade. I drank some of both and poured the extra water over my head to cool off.

Around my halfway point, Nick, Steve, and I all converged on the course. Nick had caught up to me at the same moment we passed Steve going the other direction on his way back to the finish. It seemed appropriate that all of us would share a moment on the course since we had started the triathlon journey together.

I ran as much as I could but walked some of the hills, as I was carefully monitoring myself in the heat. I concluded that it was, in fact, the most challenging 10k I'd ever done. I desperately wanted it to be over. I shuffled along, checking on other runners who were suffering in the heat and encouraging people I passed. Finally, I could see the finish area.

I tried to sprint, but I didn't have much fuel left in the tank. I ran past the big orange SBR (Swim Bike Run of Saint Louis) tent as I made the last turn, then pushed as hard as I could and ran through the Fleet Feet finish line, grinning ear to ear.

I'd done it. I'd completed my first triathlon. It hadn't been pretty, but that didn't matter. I'd conquered a whole new challenge.

My crew gathered around, and we celebrated. Katie's husband, Brian, had won the sprint course, finishing first overall. Farrell made it to the podium, too, finishing top in her age group in the Olympic distance. I was impressed by them, but it didn't overshadow the fact that I'd accomplished something I'd at one time thought unattainable. I hadn't let fear of the unknown hold me back.

I saw Teri Griege and congratulated her, not sure she even remembered me. She high-fived and told me, "Good job!" I sought out others I recognized to say "Congrats!"

The camaraderie that day blew me away. It didn't matter that I was one of the slowest athletes on the course. I was welcomed into the fold. It was a picture of sportsmanship at its finest.

As the festivities wound down, we gathered our gear and headed to our cars. Nick and I loaded the stuff and set towels in the seats before climbing in. From the dashboard, I grabbed the envelope my manager had given me the day before marked, "Open after your race."

I tore open the envelope. As I read the words from my manager, who'd also become a dear friend, my eyes welled up with tears: "I have no doubt you'll finish what you've set out to do. I'm proud of your determination to tri. You've earned it."

Along with the card was the car magnet I'd been eyeing in the store. "I'm not buying it until I've earned it," I'd told her.

Smiling, I jumped from the front seat and ran around to slap the magnet on the back of the car. Nick watched and admired the new addition to my SUV. It read "Tri."

I was officially a triathlete.

Limping with Confidence

As I transitioned from married to single, I learned to test those waters as well, encountering more people along the way who provided a sense of camaraderie or teamwork.

Almost immediately after filing for divorce, I'd begun thinking about where I'd live. I knew I wouldn't stay in the house my husband and I had bought together, for a multitude of reasons, but I had few connections in town, having lived in Saint Louis only about a year. I called a real estate agent and left a rambling message: "I don't know if you remember me, but you showed us a house about a year ago, and now I need to find one of my own, but I don't have a clue what I'm doing."

The agent, JT, did remember me and called back right away. We looked at houses off and on for a year. A solid year.

I was desperate to have my own space, but I watched a couple houses slip away. Finally, just over a year into the process, Mom and I stumbled across an open house. As soon as we walked in, we both knew we'd found my house. The timing was right, the neighborhood centered around a little lake, and the deck overlooked the water.

My offer was accepted, and I jumped through the hoops of buying a house by myself. Becoming a single homeowner was one of the most terrifying things I'd ever done, much like swimming, but my agent, JT, talked me through every step.

About a week after that first successful disaster of a triathlon, I prepared to move into my own home. The night before the closing, I finished packing and got ready for the movers to come in the morning. My ex-husband and I had already divided things up and decided who would take what.

My Pathfinder was in the garage, loaded high with the last of the things I didn't want to send with the movers. I made several trips to load my clothes into the back of the hatch. Carrying my last armload, my final trip down the stairs, I missed the last step and fell on the hard concrete floor. I yelled in pain as I sprawled onto the garage floor, with clothes and hangers scattered all around me.

Mom rushed into the garage to find me crying on the floor with a twisted ankle. She moved me to the couch—the same couch where I'd spent so many nights crying in the past year, the couch where I'd once lain under a blanket contemplating why I should ever eat again, the couch the movers would pack up and take to my new house and where I would still snuggle with my kids and reflect on how our lives had changed.

I lay on the couch, a bag of frozen peas on my ankle, debating if I should go to the emergency room.

"What am I going to do?" I whined in anguish.

"It's going to be okay. The movers will take the big stuff, and we'll do what we can tomorrow."

"No, I mean, I'm supposed to run the Chicago Marathon in three weeks! What if I go to the doctor and she says I can't run?"

Mom shook her head. I was supposed to close on my new house in less than twelve hours, but I was more concerned about running a marathon in a few weeks.

Despite the pain, I managed to get a few hours sleep. The next morning, I hobbled into the closing office. JT and my mortgage broker greeted me with a surprised, "What happened?"

I explained the fall I'd taken the night before but laughed as I told them about it. Nothing in life ever goes off without a hitch. You just have to learn to roll with the punches—or the stairs, or the waves—as the case may be.

My last few weeks of training for the Chicago Marathon that year didn't happen. I'd just moved into a new house, followed by a furniture delivery with "assembly required." My head spun from all of the effort. There wasn't much time to train even if I'd been able to run on my bruised, swollen ankle.

A few days before the marathon, after skipping my last twenty miler and having not run at all in two weeks, I set out for a short, easy jog from my new house to see if I could run at all. My ankle was sore and stiff, mildly swollen, and sporting a beautiful array of colors. I took it easy but managed to get moving. I was disappointed that I'd probably not hit the marathon goal I'd set for myself, but I was determined to head to Chicago to give it a try.

Each marathon I ran had its own story. The first and second times I ran the Chicago Marathon, I lived just blocks from the course. The third time was a couple weeks after I'd moved away. The fourth was a month post-divorce on an injured ankle.

As I ran through the familiar streets of the city that was once my home, I took in every moment. The significance of this very symbolic race struck me like a bolt of lightning. I'd accomplished so much since the days I called the Windy City home. I'd begun to face my fears and had found new confidence. I'd never let obstacles or challenges defeat me ever again. I might fall down, but I resolved to always get back up.

14: LEARNING NEW SKILLS

After the Lake Saint Louis triathlon swimming fiasco, Steve and Nick presented a strong argument. I'd survived almost a mile swim; 1.2 miles wasn't that much farther. Why not sign up for a half distance IRONMAN distance tri?

I'd faked my way through that first one. When Nick and Steve joined me in the pursuit of triathlon and both seemed to take to it naturally, I didn't want to be left behind. Though 70.3 miles is a significant haul, I was comfortable with all but 1.2 miles of it. I'd already survived most of it, even if my swimming resembled a toddler learning to doggy paddle.

"What the hell," I agreed. We researched and decided on IRONMAN® 70.3® Racine, Wisconsin. I made Steve sit next to me and hold my hand when I submitted my race entry. I also vowed I'd actually learn to swim.

Because it was January, I'd resolved, in my non-resolution-making way, that this was the year I'd learn how to swim. I was in my late thirties, and it was time to seek some much-needed assistance. Enter Andy, my swim coach.

As with so many things that happened during the blur of my divorce, I don't recall exactly how I found Andy. A customer told me about the adult swim classes at Crestview Middle School and must have mentioned Andy.

The first time I went to Crestview, I didn't take my swim gear because I only wanted to see the facility. I wasn't ready to get my feet wet, literally or figuratively. I pulled into the parking lot of the middle school and eased my car into an open space, desperately wanting a good reason to turn around and go home. I sat in my car, staring at my phone and procrastinating as long as possible. Finally, I decided it was time.

I made my way down the outdoor hallway toward the double doors to the indoor pool. Hordes of students on their way to classes chattered and laughed as they walked past me.

As I entered the pool area, I took a deep breath of the chlorine-saturated air. I tried to convince myself to act like the adult I was, but I felt smaller than the students on the middle school campus.

I spied a guy sitting in a chair near the entryway. "Are you Andy?" I asked hesitantly.

"Yeah, sure am," he replied, giving me an easy smile.

I told him my name and my situation, that I was a runner-turned-triathlete, but I needed a little help with my swim technique. Actually, I needed a lot of help with my swim technique.

I was very aware of the women gliding through the water in the pool as I recounted to Andy my experience at Lifetime Fitness, just up the road, where I'd attempted to swim some laps one morning. I'd completed only a couple laps when a man in the lane next to mine interrupted me.

"You might want to consider taking some lessons," he said.

"Yeah, I'm trying to figure this out," I replied sheepishly.

"I strongly suggest you get some lessons before you develop some bad habits," he advised.

In other words, I was terrible. As if I weren't self-conscious enough, a perfect stranger had stopped me to point out the obvious.

A few minutes later, I hopped out of the pool, grabbed a towel, and vowed never to set foot in that pool again. I was completely mortified. I'd already been aware of my deficiency, but with that, I felt completely hopeless.

When I finished my story, Andy told me he was convinced he could help me. Although I wasn't so certain, I agreed to come back the following Tuesday to give him a chance.

"Okay, that wasn't so hard," I thought to myself, walking back to the car. As much as I wanted to feel confident about what I was taking on, I felt like an imposter. It seemed pretty clear, or so I believed, that I didn't belong there, but I kept taking one step at a time.

Swim lessons, phase one, mission accomplished. I'd found an instructor.

Going Back for More

The next week when Tuesday rolled around, my nerves were on edge again. I gathered up my gear and drove to Crestview, making certain I had the ten-dollar nonmember fee in my pocket. Again, I sat in the car, reminded myself to breathe, tried to gather my courage, and simultaneously looked for an escape. I watched another swimmer emerge from her car and head inside.

I finally turned off the engine, but my brain kept running. Thoughts tumbled through my mind: "Why am I so scared to admit I don't know what I'm doing and allow someone to help me? Why do I care if I look like a fool to these women who've been swimming their entire lives? I don't even know them! I'm a runner. I don't have the first clue about pool etiquette, but how would I?"

I grabbed my keys and locked the car, threw my backpack over my shoulder, and strolled just as uneasily as the week before toward the pool.

"Hey, you came back!" Andy said cheerfully as he took my ten and pointed me toward the women's locker room. His approachability made it easier for me to keep moving forward.

A few women were in the pool, warming up and swimming laps. Others were in the locker room getting changed. I found an empty locker and shoved my stuff inside, changed out of my sweats, and put on my shiny black lycra swimsuit. Grabbing my swim cap and goggles, I made my way out to the pool deck.

Andy started the regulars off with their workout and then met me on the opposite side of the pool. As I struggled to put on my swim cap and goggles, I cautioned him, "Seriously, I don't have the first clue what I'm doing, so please try not to laugh at me too much."

Andy did laugh at me in the months ahead but never because of my swimming ability or lack thereof. He was just a cheerful soul who appreciated my humor.

"All right, the first thing you need to do is get in the water and swim to the end of the pool so I can see what we're working with," Andy instructed.

I fidgeted, adjusting my goggles, tugging at my swim cap, and delaying as long as I possibly could. Then I took a deep breath, pushed off the wall, and fought my way through the water to the end of the pool.

"Interesting," Andy said, nodding, as I grabbed the wall, gasping for air after a mere twenty-five meters. "I don't think I've ever seen anyone do that."

"That doesn't sound like a good thing," I said.

"You're a runner. Your kick is so strong that you're trying to make the rest of your body keep up with it, and you exhaust yourself in the process. Try this. Swim back to the other end but leave the kick out of it. Use only your arms to pull yourself through the water. And try to keep your head down farther. You're trying to look up in front of you too much, and that's making it harder for you to breathe, tensing up your neck and shoulders. Try to think of keeping your chin tucked into your chest even more than feels natural."

"All right." I didn't expect it to feel very different, but I was willing to give it a shot. If my legs were my strength, why would I want to take them out of the equation? But I was willing to trust the expert.

I pushed off the wall and started back to the other end. I let my legs drag behind me in the water as I slowly pulled myself through the length of the pool.

"Okay, how did that feel?" he asked as I reached the wall.

"Oh my gosh, so much better!" I exclaimed. I couldn't believe the difference those tiny changes had made.

"Good. Yeah, you looked more relaxed and not as—"

"Spastic," I finished for him.

"Well, 'tense' is what I was going to say." He smiled. "Okay, now keep those things in mind. But I also want you to think about always keeping your fingertips pointing at the bottom of the pool and your elbows up toward the sky. You can even drag your fingertips along so they skim the top of the water."

"That's a lot to remember, but I'll try."

Andy was so laid back and he put things in such easy terms that I caught on quickly. He had me do a few drills that were tricky at first, but I stuck with it. By the time I left an hour and a half later, I could swim 100 meters without stopping—and I didn't feel as if I were going to die!

Being able to swim one length of the pool without gasping for air at the end was a huge victory. I had a long way to go, but I was already getting the hang of it. I was more confident than ever that I'd be able to master this new skill.

I pressed on, still nervous and insecure, training with Andy at least once a week. Ideally, I should have been there two or three times a week, but that wasn't practical with my work and custody schedule. I did what I could reasonably commit to, and that was enough.

The other women in the pool never said much about my lack of ability. If they noticed at all, they kept it to themselves. There were some crazy good swimmers in that group, including former Olympians and record holders. To say I was intimidated was an understatement. But it helped me appreciate why newbie runners were intimidated by my marathons, and it made me look at them in a new way.

There were other triathletes who occasionally came to group swim. One was Teri Griege, amazing Teri. Though I rarely saw her there—but knowing what she had to overcome to continue swimming, biking, and running—I continued to be inspired by her courage. If she could take that on while undergoing chemo, I could overcome my insecurities about getting into the pool.

Sarah, another friend I met while sharing a pool lane one day, was so encouraging; she did her thing and never ever made me feel out of place. She was like a mother hen who looked out for me.

Along with learning to swim, I learned other valuable lessons at Crestwood. No matter where I went or what I did, I could always find good people if I looked for them. There were people who were willing to help pick me up when I needed it, who would help alleviate my fears of getting in the water.

Andy often reassured me, especially at the early lessons: "The breath will always be there."

On the first day, I'd told him I felt as if I needed to breathe with every stroke. He responded, "Okay, so breathe with every stroke if you need to. Eventually, you'll get more comfortable and realize that the breath is always there. You just have to look for it."

He was right. The more I swam and practiced the basic things he taught me, the longer I could go with my face in the water. I learned to trust that the air would be there when I needed it. "Just breathe; the air is always there." His words were like a record on repeat when I needed them.

15: VALUABLE LESSONS

On a crisp spring day after work, I'd planned to get a few miles in on the bike. I wasn't worried about distance so much as getting more comfortable with the whole idea of biking. I'd brought all my gear with me, and at the end of my shift, I changed into my new cycling clothes.

It was sunny, but there was a nip in the air, thanks to a sharp breeze. I hopped in the car and drove to the parking area at the entrance of the levee path in the valley. I got out of the car and started to prep my bike, only to see I had not one but two flat tires. "Ugh!" I said out loud to myself.

I loaded the bike back up and drove to the nearby shop where I'd bought my bike rack and other cycling supplies. I knew there was a male employee there who was nice to look at, so I didn't mind having a reason to go in.

When I opened the door, I was greeted by the cute employee's dog. "Hi, Tug," I said, petting the sweet boxer on the head with one hand while awkwardly juggling my bike with the other.

"Hey! How's it goin'?" Tug's owner asked.

"Hey! Pretty good," I said.

"What can we do for ya today?"

"Well, I was just headed out for a ride, and I had a flat. Two, actually." I wondered if my crush showed on my face.

"Oh, okay. We can get ya fixed up real quick," he said smiling.

As much as I knew about running, I felt pretty ignorant in the world of cycling. I followed him around the store as he gathered the appropriate tools to get me back on track. He put my bike up on the rack and changed the tires in the same amount of time it would have taken me to tie my shoes.

He assembled the supplies I'd need to fix a flat myself if it happened again, and I stared at him blankly. I wondered how I'd ever fix a flat myself. As he rang up my total, I handed over my credit card, making a mental note to ask someone to teach me later.

Tug followed me to the door of the shop.

"Have a good ride!" the cute boy hollered at me.

"Thanks! See ya!" I yelled over my shoulder.

I pushed open the door and managed to wrangle my bike through. I considered bailing on the whole idea of a ride as I loaded my bike. The breeze had picked up, it was chilly, and I'd lost a fair amount of time. I decided not to let the obstacles get the best of me and headed back to the levee.

It did prove to be a challenging ride, fighting the wind, but I got some miles in and learned a valuable lesson. I knew I was afraid of getting a flat tire during a race, but I also knew I needed to be able to handle the situation if it ever came up.

When I got home, I shot a message off to a group of friends, asking who could teach me how to change a bike tire. Roberto quickly volunteered. Then one of the other guys in the group offered to host a workshop for others who wanted to learn. We gathered at his house, and everyone brought food and drinks to share. My initial plea for help had turned into a party with people who continued to endear themselves to me—people who looked out for one another, took care of each other, and welcomed me into the fold.

Roberto showed all of us how to change a tire and then had all of us try on our own. I practiced changing the tire and reattaching it to my bike. The best way to keep fear at bay, I learned, was to eliminate the unknowns. I couldn't predict whether I'd ever get a flat during a race, but now I knew I could handle it if it happened.

Epic Wipeout

I immersed myself in the world of cycling. I'd upgraded the little blue Trek for a titanium road bike, trading in "Little Blue" toward the new bike and securing a loan to cover the balance. Since I'd made the extravagant purchase on Valentine's Day, I named the new bike Val.

With Val, I learned about all kinds of special gadgets to help me ride faster. Most important, I purchased clip-in pedals to increase resistance so no movement was wasted. To benefit from those special pedals, I also bought the required shoes. The shoes had a small clip on the bottom that hooked into the pedal like a little puzzle piece that clicked into place.

It took some practice to get in and out of the pedals correctly and even more practice to be efficient. It took an equal amount of concentration to learn how to twist my heel to disengage the connection. As someone not particularly coordinated, with a tendency toward clumsiness, I thought it was a good idea to learn somewhere with minimal traffic and a soft place to land in the event of a mishap.

I was still getting used to the fancy new road bike when my friend Nikki agreed to meet for a casual ride around Forest Park on a beautiful spring afternoon. I took advantage of the opportunity for some company. We met near the skating rink on the east side of the park and planned to do loops around the perimeter. The outer path measured not quite six miles, so we hoped for a couple loops to make it worthwhile in terms of mileage.

It was chilly, but the ride would provide a nice rest for my joints after the effort I'd expended the previous weekend running the two-hundred-mile Smoky Mountain Relay. Or so I thought.

"I want to hear about your relay last weekend," Nikki said as we got moving.

"Oh my gosh, it was so amazing!" I answered.

Nikki and I set off clockwise around the park. It was a slow start. I struggled to clip in and out, but after a near fall, we got going and I was able to share the details with her.

"It was more than two hundred miles through the Smoky Mountains in North Carolina. We were a team of nine, seven guys and two girls, so we each had to do four legs of the race. We had someone running from when we started on Friday morning until we finished on Saturday afternoon."

"Did you stop overnight to sleep?"

"The race kept going through the night, but we slept in the van, and the guys took turns driving from one exchange point to the next."

"That's so crazy!"

"Yeah, but it was so much fun, and the scenery was incredible!" I said. "But I had one leg that was five and a half miles straight up a mountain in the middle of the night. It was pitch dark."

"What?"

"Yeah, I was convinced I was going to run into a bear."

"Did you?" she asked.

"No! I would have peed my pants!"

We both laughed.

"When we got to my last leg of the race, we passed the race director, so the course wasn't even marked yet. I got completely lost in a ravine, and one of my teammates had to come into the woods to find me."

"Wow!"

"But I wouldn't trade the experience for anything. I got to hang out with awesome people in a beautiful place and do what I love. It was really hard, but it was worth it. Our team ended up coming in second place."

"That's so great!"

"Yeah," I smiled. "I really needed that."

Nikki and I continued to chat while we rode. The conversation shifted to her job as a nurse and my life a single working mom training for endurance sports.

We soaked up the sunshine and the scenery, climbed the hill by the dinosaurs outside the Saint Louis Science Center and whizzed past the zoo. It was rush hour on Friday. Traffic was heavy, making the safety of the bike path that much more comforting. We used gravity to our advantage as we coasted down the hill that ran parallel to Skinker Boulevard. We were headed north at a pretty good pace with the breeze blowing through our helmets.

As we approached the big entrance to the park at Forsyth Boulevard, we spotted a crosswalk directly ahead. In my mind, I planned to cruise right on through to the other side and continue on the bike path. But then I registered the "Don't Walk" sign and realized we didn't have the right-of-way. We needed to stop immediately, but I was going too fast.

What happened next seemed to occur in an instant and in slow motion at the same time. I was aware I needed to stop, but I couldn't remember how to detach my feet from the bike pedals. A crash was inevitable, it was just a matter of where it would happen. Noting the lush, soft grass to my right and several people and gravel only ten yards ahead, I made a split-second decision. Almost instantly, I flew toward the ground and hit the grass. Hard.

For a moment, I lay there stunned, then I took inventory. I didn't think I'd broken anything, at least not anything important. When the shock wore off, I began to laugh. I laughed so hard that no sound came out.

I looked up to see Nikki standing over me, a look of shock and concern on her face. Once she was certain I was laughing rather than crying, she started laughing, also. After a few minutes of rolling on the ground in hysterics, I managed to untangle myself from my bike, and Nikki helped me to my feet. Anyone who happened to be on Skinker Boulevard at 5:40 p.m. that day surely went home and told the story of the epic wipeout they'd witnessed.

Sometimes things like that happen in life. You're skipping along, thinking everything is hunky-dory, and then suddenly you're screaming, "Mayday! Mayday! Man down!"

That episode humbled me, but I was okay with that. I'd learned a valuable lesson. I'd been going too fast, not paying attention, and I got slapped in the face with what could go wrong. Ultimately, when near catastrophe struck, I was able to laugh about it, pick myself up, and keep right on going. I had to dislodge about a square foot of dirt from my cycling shoes first, but I got right back in the saddle.

Sometimes life hands you a good old-fashioned face plant. What are ya gonna do about it?

Ditching the Training Wheels

With the newer, fancier bike and having registered for a half distance IRONMAN, I was ready to start logging some real bike miles. I needed more experience than the comfortable recreational rides. I rarely ventured off the levee path alone. It was flat, not heavily trafficked, and no cars were allowed. I was still so unsure of all bike etiquette on the road that I wanted to ride with other people who could show me the ropes, but my time with my kids and retail schedule rarely afforded me that luxury.

I'd heard about a women's ride that met at a bike shop in the valley, so one morning, I summoned my courage and decided to check it out. Riding with veteran cyclists wasn't quite as scary as learning to swim; at least on my bike, I could fake it. I didn't have all the best gear and didn't understand all the lingo, but riding a bike was like, well, riding a bike—and that much I knew how to do.

I pulled into the parking lot and glanced around, expecting to see lots of women with bikes. Instead, I saw one guy and that was it. It was just after nine in the morning, and the shop didn't open until ten, so I couldn't go in and ask about it. I heaved a sigh of insecurity, got out of the car, and decided to ask the guy if he knew about the women's ride.

"Hey, do you know anything about a women's ride that's supposed to meet here?"

"Yeah," he said, swinging his head up from his bike and looking around, "They're usually here by now. I'm not really sure what's going on."

"Thanks," I said, hoping that the mix of relief and disappointment I felt wasn't apparent in my voice. "I'm a pretty new cyclist, so I was looking forward to riding with other people."

"How far are you planning to go?" he asked.

"I don't know, maybe twenty-five. I'm supposed to be training for a half distance IRONMAN that's in a few months, so I need to get my miles up, but I'm still figuring out this bike thing."

"Well," he said, "if you're up for a few more miles, you're welcome to ride along with me."

"Are you sure? How fast do you ride?

"Oh, ya know, whatever, like seventeen to eighteen, " he said.

I was pretty confident he was downplaying his abilities so I wouldn't feel bad.

"I don't want to hold you back."

"It's really no problem," he said.

"If you don't mind me tagging along, I'd love to ride with someone who knows what they're doing."

"Sure, you're fine!" he smiled. "We'll go get you some miles."

"I'm Lindsey, by the way." He shook my hand and told me his name. He said "Greg," but I heard "Grey."

After checking tires and gearing up, we were off and riding. He led me out of the valley and up Wild Horse Creek Road, where he said he'd wait for me at the top of the hill. As promised, he was there when I got to the top, breathing heavily.

"Not bad," he said. "You ready for a little more?"

"As ready as I'll ever be," I said, flashing him a look of uncertainty. He grinned, and we took off.

He could, and did, ride circles around me. I'd struggle up a hill, huffing and puffing, and he'd stick close to me, weaving back and forth, going up, coming back down, encouraging me the entire way. I noticed that each of his thighs was about as big in diameter as my whole body.

"Don't forget to look around and enjoy the view," he said, speeding past me.

Despite my instability on the bike, I did look around, and the scenery was incredible. I felt as if I were riding my bike on top of the world.

We rode up and down the winding, hilly roads, past long white fences and fields of grazing horses. He was impressed with my determination and perseverance, while I appreciated his support and expertise. I told him stories about running, and he told me about cycling races in the mountains. It occurred to me that the hills I was suffering on, he could ride in his sleep, backwards and blindfolded.

He pointed out interesting landmarks. I simply tried to keep my breathing at a normal rate. I was holding him back, but he seemed to genuinely enjoy my company and my stories as much as I appreciated his.

We rode all the way to a gas station near Six Flags. He hopped off his bike, leaned it against the building, and went inside to buy a turkey sandwich. I stayed with the bikes and pulled a Gu and a packet of Sports Beans out of my pocket.

"You sure you don't need anything from inside?" he asked.

"Nah, I'm fine. What could possibly be better than Gu?" I joked.

After we'd devoured our snacks, we began the return trek to the valley. He took me a different route back that was also beautiful, and we talked more while we rode. We were an unlikely pair, as I knew he could have left me in the dust, but he never did. Instead he rode ahead a few times, then patiently came back to make sure I didn't miss a turn. About four hours after we'd set out, we coasted back into the bike shop parking lot. I was a sweaty, tired, hungry mess.

We traded numbers, and I thanked him for tolerating me. He laughed and took off on his bike to ride a few more miles. Without me to slow him down, he'd probably ride double what we'd accomplished in half the time. And thus began my friendship with a guy I met in a parking lot and called "Grey." He became my cycling tutor and was always ready to slow down to help me build my mileage—and my confidence.

Braking Downhill

Going downhill very fast on a bike terrified me. One day, my friend Steve wanted to ride some hills, so he came over to my house, and we jumped on our bikes. The joy of having a training partner who was both faster than me and better prepared was that I could follow along and let him lead the way. The flip side, however, was that I never knew what challenging situations Steve would present.

Usually, I was afraid of the uphill battles I'd have to fight. He'd warn me ahead of time where I needed to switch gears to be ready for a monster hill. When we went up steep grades, the lactic acid burned my quads while my lungs felt as if they might explode. Occasionally, it was the downhills that became my foe.

On that particular day, we had just left my neighborhood when we happened upon my friend Greg. He was always humble to the core, but the dude could ride a bike like nobody's business. Steve and I rode with Greg for a while, but I didn't want to hold him back, so I made sure he knew it was okay to take off and leave us behind. On the other hand, I required Steve to stay with me. As we all took off down Woods Road, the guys zipped on ahead of me, flying down the hill. I was timid, so I took my time.

When I finally met them at the bottom, I said, "There's something wrong with my brakes. They're making a weird noise."

We took off again and somewhere along the way, we lost Greg, or he lost us, but I made Steve stick close by on the next big hill so he could hear my brakes. He rode to the bottom of the hill and up to the top of the next climb well ahead of me, but he waited for me at a crossroads so we could decide where we'd go next.

"I think I need new brakes," I said when I caught up to him and unclipped at the stop sign.

He took his glucometer out of his pack to check his blood sugar. "Actually, I think you need to go faster," he said, ribbing me good-naturedly. He looked up at me with his usual Steve grin.

I laughed. "But seriously, my brakes wouldn't be that loud just from using them a little, would they?"

"You're not using them a little; you're using them a lot." He grinned again.

From that point on, it became clear I was a big chicken with a huge fear of crashing. I preferred to take my time going downhill, which was okay with me. I'd had enough friends end up with road rash and concussions that I knew I didn't want that to happen to me.

Fortunately, after all was said and done, Steve was a patient riding partner who always waited for me at the next stop.

Eventually, I learned to let off the brakes a little at a time. I never zoomed down the hills fearlessly the way he did, but I started to let go.

16: PUTTING IT ALL TOGETHER

The summer of 2013 presented this new single mom with the challenge of figuring out what to do with the kids when I had to work or train. They were enrolled in day camps, so I trained on days when they were there. My shifts at the store were typically scheduled when the kids were with their dad. Occasionally, I hired a sitter.

Fortunately, my first attempt at a half distance IRONMAN distance tri was over a weekend when the kids were with their dad. After work on Friday, I set off for Wisconsin to meet Steve and Nick, who'd driven up earlier in the day. They helped me bring my bike and the rest of my gear into the hotel, where we watched garbage TV and relaxed before the big weekend ahead.

On Saturday morning, we loaded our bikes and headed for the beach where all things IRONMAN were located. At check-in, we ran into several other friends who'd joined us from Saint Louis. Some were first-timers, others vets, but we were all filled with anticipation for a race that was a big deal. We got our race bracelets and gear, dropped off our bikes in the transition area, and hit the beach.

It was a gorgeous day for building sandcastles, but that wasn't on our agenda. Several of us had decided to go for a practice swim to test the Lake Michigan waters. Most of us were embarking on new territory, as this was our first race of such a distance, and we were nervous and excited but mostly fearful of the unknown.

Not surprising on such a sunny Saturday, the beach was packed with families, interspersed with triathletes shaking out nerves for the big event of the weekend. The water was a perfect temperature and smooth as glass. As I waded out to where my friends huddled in a group, I could clearly see the bottom of the lake and the white line that had been laid for athletes to follow the swim course.

"I can totally do this," I thought to myself, smiling. "It'll be just like the pool!"

I submerged my body in the waters of Lake Michigan to get used to the water temperature. We weren't planning to do the full swim course, just a short swim in open water to prepare. "Here goes," I thought as I adjusted my goggles on my face, and off I went. I followed the white line and breathed every few strokes on alternating sides. I even practiced *sighting*, catching a glimpse of something in the distance in the direction of travel.

When I came to a group of feet I recognized in a huddle, I popped up and sprayed water with my open hand over Nick.

"Lindsey learned how to swim!" I hollered. I was excited and energized to feel that this was going to be a piece of cake. But I should have known Lake Michigan can be temperamental. It can, and often does, change overnight.

We'd already received reports of a drastic shift in conditions as we drove to the course the next morning, but I was still optimistic. I'd decided the day before, doing the practice swim sans wetsuit, that I was going to race without it as well.

The air was mild, but a front that had moved in overnight had brought cooler water, large gray clouds, and churning waves. When we saw the waves and learned that the water temperature had dropped significantly, everyone decided that wetsuits were absolutely necessary. Everyone knew it. Everyone except me.

I wasn't comfortable in my wetsuit. Despite many trials, I still felt as if it were choking me. I went back and forth about what to do as we continued our race prep, loading water bottles onto bikes, setting out gear, and visiting the Port-O-Potty.

An announcement came over the loudspeaker that the transition area would close in ten minutes. I had to decide whether to wear my wetsuit before we made the mile walk to the start.

I looked at my friends in their wetsuits and decided to leave my wetsuit with my bike and the rest of my gear. It was, perhaps, not the smartest idea, but I was doing things the best way I knew how.

The benefit of the wetsuit, aside from keeping a person warm by acting as insulation in water cooler than body temperature, is that it creates buoyancy in the water. The idea is that swimmers don't have to work as hard if they're lifted higher in the water. However, considering that the wetsuit made me feel as if I was constantly fighting against it, I thought my choice to leave it behind seemed valid—until we made our way to the start, and I counted on one hand the athletes not wearing one.

The sky was no longer the perfect blue of the day before. It was filled with blustery, fast-moving, angry-looking gray clouds. The water was no longer smooth as glass. Instead, the waves were enormous and hostile. How was I going to swim in that?

I didn't have a lot of time to think about it. As soon as I arrived at the start, Tracy saw me and said, "Our corral is about to line up! Go jump in the water quick, so it won't be such a shock to your system!"

In my tri shorts and top, I struggled through the sand and made my way out into the water. I felt every person on the beach turn to watch me, all wondering what the crazy girl was thinking by attempting the swim with no wetsuit.

The water was freezing, and the waves crashing on me made it impossible to keep my balance. The way I stumbled around, I was certain I appeared intoxicated. I reconsidered my decision, but my wetsuit was a mile down the beach in the closed transition area, so it was no longer an option.

A rumor quickly spread that the race officials were considering canceling the swim leg of the event. I silently prayed that wouldn't happen. As much as I didn't want to participate in a swim like the one before us, I knew my disappointment would be greater if I didn't get a shot at the whole race. I'd signed up to do a swim, bike, and run—70.3 miles, no less. It was happening, so it was time to face it.

I joined Tracy at the back of the women in our age group. We both sought only to survive the experience and positioned ourselves accordingly. At the front were the swimmers who had a shot at placing, then the strong swimmers who could hold their own, then the mediocre swimmers, then weak swimmers, and finally those of us who swam only because we had to.

"I'm going to get out there however I can," Tracy said, indicating the buoy out in the water where we would turn to swim parallel to the shore. "Then I'll try to swim as best I can."

"Yep, that's my plan, too. But I think real swimming might be a lost cause. I'll get through it whatever way I can."

A Kelly Clarkson song played over the loudspeaker, and I grabbed onto the lyrics in that moment: "What doesn't kill you makes you stronger." I knew I'd come out of the water stronger, somehow. I tried to stand tall, to remember how far I'd come, but my doubts grew like the waves, chipping away at my self-confidence. And then it was our turn.

We marched under the big inflatable start line, felt the chilly sand under our feet give way to even chillier water, and made our way toward the big orange buoy. "Getting out there will be the hardest part," I tried to reassure myself, though I suspected the whole swim might be nearly impossible.

The Lake Saint Louis tri flashed in my mind as I sidestroked my way to the buoy. I struggled to breathe with the waves crashing on my face. It was a comfort to know Tracy was somewhere nearby, even if I couldn't distinguish her from anyone else in the chaos.

As the group rounded the buoy and headed south, parallel to the crowd on the sandy beach, it became much like trying to swim in a washing machine. We were tossed up, down, and all over the place. I put my face in the water in an attempt to swim as I'd been taught. I tried to breathe, but I sputtered and gagged. I felt as if the water thrashed my limbs whatever way it wanted, robbing me of any control. I gave up swimming like a triathlete and went back to the sidestroke just to stay alive.

Inside my head, I began a massive pity party. "This isn't how it was supposed to be! I learned how to swim for this, and now I don't even get to do that. This is crap."

The waves were insane; I could have sworn each one was bigger than the last. With one stroke, I was five feet higher than the person next to me, and then seconds later, she was up and I was down.

There was ample course support in the water, with kayaks we could hold on to if need be, Coast Guard boats, and every other size of vessel between. I was conflicted, wanting to stop and hang on to rest, but I knew if given the option to quit, it would be so much easier for me to say, "Yeah, okay, I'm done" than to continue with the madness of fighting the waves. To quit the swim would be to quit the entire race.

I slowly pressed on, and my mental pity party continued as well. I thought about the lyrics to a song from my training playlist about feeling overwhelmed by waves of doubt and drowning in fear before finding the faith to overcome.

At around the halfway mark, I started to push the doubts out of the way. The whining in my head turned into a different voice. I started to think to myself, "The conditions aren't ideal today, but you can either keep being a big baby about it, or you can suck it up and at least try to swim the way Andy taught you." In that moment, I put my face in the water and began to swim like a swimmer.

I heard the song again, the lyrics reminding me that I had everything I needed right there inside me. I didn't have to be afraid. I just needed to have faith.

It was still really ugly. The waves tossed us around like beach balls in a hurricane. I could breathe only on the right side. The waves rolled in from the left, and if I turned that way, I sucked in a mouthful of lake water instead of air.

I had to make do with the hand I'd been dealt, so I swam. I swam as if I were fighting for my life. At some point, I started looking like the swimmer I'd learned to be because I made the choice to stop doubting myself and trust that I could do it.

I wondered what I'd been waiting for. With each stroke, I pushed the doubts farther behind me, and I swam. Eventually, I sighted the last buoy I had to reach before the turn toward the beach and propelled myself toward it through the relentless waves. After what felt like an exhausting eternity, I made the turn back to the beach.

The huge waves crashed into the retaining wall and bounced back at us, which made it an even bigger struggle. I was almost there. So close had never seemed so far away, but I kept going. Stroke, stroke, stroke, breathe. And then I felt the sand beneath my toes. It took my whole body—arms, legs, and everything else—to drag myself from that water toward the transition area. I pulled the goggles from my face and felt the puffy circles around my eyes.

Volunteers on the beach helped athletes remove their wetsuits. One of them looked at me and said, "Wow! No wetsuit? That's hardcore!"

I offered a weak smile and a slight nod, or at least I tried to. If I'd had the ability to speak in that moment, I'd have responded, "No, not hardcore, just really stupid." But the fact remained, I'd done it.

I transitioned and went out for fifty-six miles on the bike through the Wisconsin countryside. It was bumpy but uneventful. If I didn't get a flat, I'd be fine. The last couple miles of the bike course overlapped with the run course. When I started seeing runners, I knew I was safe. Even if I got a flat, I was close enough to run my bike back to transition.

By the time I started the run, the clouds had cleared and the sun had warmed the air dramatically. It was humid and hot. I knew I had to run smart. It was a half marathon, so I was confident that even if I had to walk some, I could finish.

I ran, I walked, I drank water. I poured water on my head and ran through any sprinkler I saw. I said hi to friends I passed on the course and smiled at everyone. The end was within reach. I thought about how hard the whole thing had been, but I had no doubt that I was going to finish.

About six and a half hours after I stood on the beach questioning my abilities, I crossed the finish line after 70.3 miles, finishing with my arms raised and a smile on my face. I was Half-Iron, but I was all heart.

In a field of about 2,500 athletes, I'd been one of only a handful of people to tackle that swim without a wetsuit. I was one of even fewer to finish. Later, I learned that one of my friends had thrown up in the water and been forced to quit. I was told by triathletes who'd completed ocean swims that July 21, 2013, in Lake Michigan was the hardest swim they'd ever done.

When the celebrated Teri, who was also in Racine for that race, learned what I'd accomplished, she said, "If you can do that swim with no wetsuit, you can do *any* swim."

I'd finally started to believe that might be true. All it took was proving it to myself and having some faith.

17: DITCHING EXCUSES

I knew I'd been incredibly fortunate to find myself in relationships with people who wanted to help me along my journey, and I often felt overwhelmed with gratitude toward them. Teri Griege was one of these special people.

After her initial visit to Fleet Feet, when I first met the force that was Teri, I somehow found myself under her wing. She invited me to Fit & Fab parties at her house, and I joined her Powered by Hope team that participated in Pedal the Cause, a bike ride to raise money for cancer research. I was surprised to learn we went to the same church and was equally surprised at how genuinely happy she seemed to see me whenever we ran into each other. She always remembered me, and she quickly secured a place of admiration in my heart.

One late summer evening while I was working at the store, Teri came in with her daughter, Kati, who needed some new running shoes. I set to work helping Kati find the right pair of shoes and enjoyed talking with both of them. They sat on the bench in front of me as I sat cross-legged on the floor, gathering information from Kati about her needs. When I returned from the back room with several pairs of shoes, we talked while I adjusted Kati's footwear, chatting about how hard Racine 70.3 had been with the huge waves during the hardest swim ever, the bumps on the bike course, and the heat of the run.

While Kati went outside to try out a pair of shoes on the sidewalk, Teri asked, "So, how's everything going? Are you training for anything else?"

"Well, I kinda took a break after Racine, but I'm signed up to do Lake Saint Louis again."

She nodded as I continued, "Farrell is really trying to convince me to go to Arizona with her and some other friends in November to volunteer at IRONMAN Arizona so we can register for the race the following year. But that's just crazy. I mean, I'll probably go volunteer because I think it would be a cool experience, but I can't do an IRONMAN."

"Why not?" Teri asked.

"How would I train for that? I'm still getting used to being a single mom, and I just . . ." I knew the words *I can't* didn't exist to the phenomenal woman sitting before me.

"Lindsey," she said, looking straight at me, "what are you really afraid of? Sometimes you just have to go on faith that it's all going to work out. Just think about it."

I let out a sigh as Kati rejoined us with a smile on her face. "Yeah, I like these!" she said.

I boxed up Kati's new shoes, and as I said goodbye to them, I knew I was going to Arizona. I knew I was going to volunteer and that I was going to sign up for IRONMAN Arizona 2014. How could I ever say no to Teri, the woman who'd completed IRONMAN Kona while battling cancer?

Run Aid Station #5

So, I bought a plane ticket. Farrell was chomping at the bit to get back to Tempe for another shot at IRONMAN, and she wanted to bring an entourage with her. She'd done her research, and she knew that for first-timers and anyone who wanted to qualify for the IRONMAN World Championships, the IRONMAN Arizona course was considered fast and flat. She also knew that fast and flat didn't mean easy. It was all relative.

However, because of IRONMAN Arizona's reputation, it was a tough race to get into. Every year, registration sold out within minutes of opening online, but since every IRONMAN event also needed hundreds of volunteers to run smoothly, the best way to get into the race was to earn a spot through volunteering.

Farrell put together a group of interested people and emailed us all the information with the link to sign up. We all chose the same volunteer spot so we could work together: Run Aid Station #5.

When the November weekend arrived, I met Farrell at the airport. Along with Adrienne, another friend who'd previously worked at Fleet Feet, we boarded a plane to Phoenix. The three of us were going to stay at Farrell's aunt and uncle's house.

Our group included Ron and Mark, a couple of triathletes Farrell worked out with who rented a car and acted as our chauffeurs. Farrell's good friends Kelly and Sheila, newlyweds, were both fairly new to triathlons. Kelly was ready to go the full distance. Sheila, who was fine with the half distance, was on the hook as support and our team photographer.

On Saturday, Farrell, Adrienne, and I went for a short run on the streets of Phoenix. The elevation made it tougher than back home, so we cut it short after a few miles.

Ron and Mark picked us up, and we drove to Tempe for our first look at IRONMAN Village, a virtual town consisting of canopies, trailers, tents, and orange makeshift fencing. The transition areas already contained piles of athletes' gear bags and a sea of bicycles organized on racks. We wandered through the maze of booths, trying samples of nutrition products and looking for bargains. Mark purchased a pair of shoes and contemplated a helmet. I bought a new pair of goggles at the suggestion of the veteran triathletes.

We entered the merchandise tent, and I was overwhelmed by the IRONMAN gear: T-shirts, jackets, tri kits, hats, towels, bags, coffee mugs, Christmas ornaments. They had everything imaginable. I'd never been one to even wear my free T-shirt before I finished a race and earned it. I was there to look, nothing more. However, I did find a T-shirt that read #yougotchicked. *Chicked* is an athlete's way of saying beat by a girl. I decided I needed it as a reminder of having found my strength again.

After spending the day immersed in the world of IRONMAN, we got fancy and went out for the evening in Scottsdale. Kelly and Sheila met the rest of us at a sushi restaurant for dinner, drinks, and conversation. After dinner, we walked around Scottsdale and found another place for drinks before retiring to our separate sleeping quarters for the night.

The next morning, some of the group went to watch the start of IRONMAN. As a single mom with a weekend off in Arizona, I opted to take advantage of the opportunity to enjoy a little time to myself. After enjoying the luxury of sleeping in, I filled my hydration pack, a vest with a bladder for fluids to make for easy carrying and access. I asked Farrell's relatives for directions to the closest trail, laced up my running shoes, and set off to the Phoenix hills. Conveniently, there was a mountain at the back of their neighborhood. I headed there intending to climb it, venture down the other side, locate the tunnel under the highway, and get to the summit of Piestewa Peak.

I reached the edge of the neighborhood—a mountain rising right out of someone's back yard—located the trailhead, and started to climb. Initially, I was full of energy and adrenaline, but it didn't take long for me to realize I could run only the downhills and flats. I had to hike uphill.

I slowly made my way upward, and since it wasn't too high a peak, I arrived at the top fairly quickly. I stared at the expanse before me. Trails went off in every direction. There were so many options and so much blue sky, and I had all day with only one mission: to get lost and then find my way back.

I ran down a path lined with cacti and tumbleweeds and noticed a coyote in the distance. At the base of the hill, I ran along the highway, looking for the entrance to the passage underneath. After searching in both directions, I found the tunnel, passed through, and discovered the park entrance to Piestewa Peak on the other side. I was grateful for the welcome sight of water fountains and restrooms.

The sun was high in the sky and beat down intensely. I'd gone through most of my water, so I refilled and began to climb. It was a slow vertical process. I relished the sun, the blue sky, fresh air, and incredible views.

I stopped near the top to take a picture, looked at my phone, and noted the date. It had been exactly twelve years since I'd last seen my dad alive, twelve years since that day in Union Station when I'd said goodbye to him. I took a quivery breath. Tears filled my eyes, and one slipped down my cheek. How had so much time crawled by since the last time he hugged me, and yet it had also passed in a flash?

I stood there remembering everything about our last goodbye and everything that had happened since. I could still smell his combination of aftershave and peanut butter. I could still feel the soft suede of his dark-green sportscoat.

"I miss you, Dad," I whispered into the air. "I don't know what I'm doing here, but I know you're with me every step of the way."

I took my time and eventually arrived at the summit. I snapped some photos, then sat and savored the peace that washed over me before beginning my descent back to reality. I got lost again on the return trip, multiple times really, but I loved every minute of it. It was in the getting lost that I found part of myself.

I was sitting on top of the hill at the edge of the neighborhood when my phone rang. Farrell was calling to check in.

"Hey," I answered.

"Hey, where are you?" she asked.

"Sitting up here on top of this mountain enjoying the view."

"It sounds windy," she said.

"Yeah, there's a nice breeze, but it's perfect. The sun is intense, though."

"No kidding. I hope you wore sunscreen. Are you planning to come back?" she teased.

"Yeah, I'm close. What time do we need to leave?" I said.

"I think the guys are coming to pick us up in about an hour, so we have plenty of time before we report for duty."

"Okay, I'm just a few minutes away. I'll head back, and I'm going to need a shower."

"Okay, we're here. I might take a nap. See you soon," she said

"Yep! Bye."

I stood, brushed off the dust, and took a deep breath as I memorized the view. Then I jogged down the hill that eventually gave way to the street that led me back to the house. I'd covered around fourteen miles over several hours. It had been slow and steady, beautiful and peaceful—exactly what I'd needed.

I cleaned up and put on my comfy clothes, ready to volunteer in the Arizona desert that night. Ron and Mark picked us up, and we all made our way to our volunteer station. As we walked, we cheered on the athletes running the course right next to us. It was surreal. They'd been up since early morning, had swum 2.4 miles, biked 112, and were in the middle of running a marathon. I was amazed that the human body was capable of such a feat.

We located the tables designated as Run Aid Station #5, checked in, and we took over for the volunteers ending the previous shift. We restocked paper cups filled with pretzels, chips, water, Gatorade, and other items and assisted the runners with whatever they needed.

But we also had plenty of time to play and be silly. Due to the layout of the course, the athletes had to run past us four times. As the evening wore on, we began to recognize some of the runners, and they won our hearts, particularly the ones who wore their struggles like a badge of honor: the gray-haired man, the overweight girl, the military amputee. I was inspired by their determination and perseverance. They made me look at myself and wonder what was stopping me. Right then, I had no answer.

Our group volunteered alongside another group of friends from Albuquerque. I chatted with Marc, a single dad, who encouraged me to give an IRONMAN a shot.

"You'll love it," he declared.

When our shift was over, the supervisor pulled us into a huddle and put a bracelet around each of our wrists. The bracelets indicated we'd earned the right to sign up for IRONMAN Arizona 2014. I knew the instant that bracelet was put on my wrist that I was going to attempt the seemingly impossible. I had no clue how I was going to do it, but I knew I had to try.

We were tired from a long day, and we had to line up early the next morning to register for IRONMAN Arizona 2014 before our flight back to Saint Louis, so we returned to our temporary homes and crashed for a few hours. After a very early awakening, we headed back to IRONMAN Village once more, credit cards in hand.

The line was long when we arrived, and it moved at a turtle's pace. Our anticipation grew as we inched along. Athletes from the previous day limped around us proudly on their way to the merchandise tent to purchase a coveted and well-deserved finisher's jacket.

When I got to the front of the line to hand over the $850 registration fee, equivalent to an entire paycheck, I heard a familiar Southern drawl and turned to see the face of Judy—Dallas Judy! When I'd met her on a bus several years earlier and she'd predicted I'd sign up for an IRONMAN, I was absolutely sure that the moment we were in would never happen—and I certainly didn't expect her to be present for it.

"Oh my gosh, Judy!" I half yelled.

"Lindsey! My goodness! Hi!" she said from behind her volunteer station.

"Are you registered for next year, too?" I asked excitedly.

"I sure am!" she said. "Let's get you registered, too!"

I nervously provided the necessary information, handing over my ID and credit card. Then I signed on the dotted line, and it was a done deal. She printed a confirmation and met me at the end of the table to congratulate me with a hug. She introduced me to her boyfriend, Adam, who took a photo of the two of us with our registrations for IRONMAN Arizona 2014 in hand. Both of us were beaming.

Under my smile, I was terrified, but it was so exhilarating. I'd overcome my self-doubts and put aside my excuses. I was going to give it my all at IRONMAN Arizona 2014. As scary as it was, I'd never been so proud of myself.

18: TAKING CHANCES

I continued my weekly sessions with my therapist, Jen. We took a hard, introspective look at my divorce, the abuse I'd faced, and my unhealthy relationship with food. When I felt out of control, I stopped eating because food was the one thing I could control. I tortured my body and punished myself because I thought I deserved it. Jen was determined to help me get to the bottom of how and why I'd landed there.

Ultimately, I understood that I didn't expect people to treat me well, so I tolerated whatever behavior they threw my way. I'd believed so many lies about myself that I no longer knew who I truly was. I was convinced I was inadequate, and I'd compromised myself to try to fit someone else's expectations of me. Sometime early in young adulthood, I'd succumbed to the belief that I didn't deserve to be loved. My spirit had been broken.

I'd learned to hide my emotions and my insecurities, so exposing my vulnerability, even to Jen, was excruciating. But to become an authentic version of myself, I continued to do the hard work, showing up week after week to sit on Jen's couch. Clutching a pillow on my lap, I poured out my heart and soul to her.

For the first time in my adult life, I was alone. Being unattached to another person was strange initially, and sometimes it got lonely. Jen urged me to "sit in the loneliness."

It was especially hard when the kids were at their dad's house. I gave myself permission to sit in the car a few extra minutes until I was ready to face walking into a big, empty house. At those times, I often decided to sleep on the couch, rather than drag myself up the stairs to the cavern of silence and see all their beds with no one in them.

I learned to be comfortable with myself and my feelings. It wasn't realistic to always be happy Lindsey, so I tore down the wall of numbness and started to let others see my emotions behind the mask.

I struggled to find my identity as an individual rather than tagging myself with labels like daughter, sister, wife, mother—labels that had always attached me to someone else. I was Lindsey.

I was emphatic that I didn't want to be married again, but if I was ever going to find a partner in the future, I knew he needed to accept me for the messy, broken, independent, work-in-progress I was.

My dating life was not much to talk about. I refused to try online dating, much to the disappointment of my coworkers. I'd heard too many horror stories from friends who'd gone down that road, and I wasn't going to put myself through additional trauma. For me, it was going to happen naturally or not at all.

I occasionally went out with men, but things rarely progressed past a date or two. I really enjoyed my friends when I wasn't busy being a single, working mom. I enjoyed easy laughter and a cold beer with friends who shared common interests or a night of karaoke with the Fleet Feet gang. If I needed the company of a male companion, I'd text Steve to see if he wanted to go for a run or catch a movie. Steve had struggles of his own. Not long before we'd met, he'd told his family he was gay, and I knew he wanted nothing more from me than friendship. At a time when I was learning to trust men, Steve was a safe and good companion.

In December of 2013, I left work on a Sunday and was on my way to my kids' school Christmas program. As I made the short trip to their school, it dawned on me that I really wanted someone I could count on to go with me to events, someone I could depend on to fall in step beside me. Someone who understood how exhausting it was to put on a brave face and be strong all the time. I wanted someone to help me carry the weight—not take the weight from me, just help me carry it—and tell me to set it down and take a break when I needed one.

I felt feisty. I pulled out my phone before walking into the school and tapped out a Facebook post: "Quick, I need a friend-date for an event that starts in eighteen minutes. First person to respond is the lucky winner. Go!"

Once inside the school, I lost all phone reception. I took a deep breath and prepared to sit alone at a school where I was a pioneer of sorts, the first single mom of the bunch. Not only was I alone, but I knew my ex-husband would be there with his entire family, who were not particularly warm toward me. I understood why they didn't accept me, but it still felt bitterly painful and lonely.

I chatted with other parents and sat smiling at my kids as they performed. It was the holidays, after all, and I was supposed to be cheerful. In some ways, I was, but I also felt incredibly awkward and really wanted to get the hell out of there.

When it was finally over, I saw my kids at a table with their dad, grandparents, aunt, uncle, and cousins. Summoning all my courage and walked over to give the kids a hug. They threw their arms around my waist; no one else acknowledged me. It was okay. I'd prepared for it, and I needed attention only from the kids anyway. I didn't linger. I told my children what a great job they'd done and then hurried back to the car.

As soon as I stepped outside, my phone buzzed with notifications. I sat in my car reading a couple texts from friends as well as comments on my earlier post. An old friend from elementary school had commented that he couldn't make it, but he suggested the name of another classmate of ours who lived in Saint Louis and was single. I remembered the guy and sent him a friend request. I wasn't sure if he'd even remember who I was. What did I have to lose? Then I drove to Katrina's new apartment for an all-girls Christmas party.

At Kat's place, I was delighted to find several of my Fleet Feet girlfriends. We drank spiked hot chocolate, dropped a chihuahua into a pie, and laughed until our stomachs hurt.

As the evening wound down, I checked my phone. That old classmate, Brian, had accepted my request, and we began messaging. He was engaging and hilarious; I looked forward to his responses before they came. He was a single dad with a little boy, worked at Washington University, and also liked to run but not competitively.

It was only a matter of days before we started trying to figure out when we could meet. It took some planning with our mismatched kids and work schedules, but we finally landed on a time to meet for drinks on a Monday evening after I got off work.

On December 23, only a few weeks after I friended Brian on Facebook, I helped close the store, quickly changed clothes, and drove to our planned meeting spot in Clayton. I walked inside to find Brian sitting at the bar. He stood, we exchanged greetings, and then we moved to a table by the window.

As we talked, he made me laugh, and it felt comfortable. I knew within minutes that I could fall in love with this handsome man with a dry sense of humor. I pushed fears aside and melted into the exhilaration of the moment.

We were the only people left in J. Buck's when the server told us she had to close out our tab. It seemed early for a bar to shut down. We agreed that, with our limited opportunities to spend time together, we'd make the most of the time we had.

I noticed black fuzz on the sleeve of his cream-colored sweater, so I reached over to remove it.

"You had a fuzz," I explained.

"Oh, it's from my, um, my . . ." he hesitated, trying to find the word. I just smiled at him.

"Scarf," he said a moment later, shaking his head, embarrassed. "It's from my scarf."

I laughed that *scarf* was the word he hadn't been able to come up with, and my heart inflated. He was as smitten as I was. I didn't know where we were headed, but it didn't matter. I was happy simply being with him, and I knew that we had lots of adventures and laughter ahead of us.

Healing and Reinjury

Early on, I wanted to be transparent with Brian. I saw our relationship going somewhere, so I wanted to be completely honest with him about who I was and what he was getting into.

As the great blizzard of 2014 took aim at Missouri, we knew we'd get socked with snow, so I proposed getting snowed in together. I stocked up on ingredients to cook all kinds of meals and other essentials for our coming days being trapped in the house.

On Saturday night, we took in the lights of the Botanical Garden. As we were leaving, the snow began to fall, and by Sunday morning, we were buried under more than a foot of the white stuff. We spent the day watching movies, cooking, playing Scrabble, and having a great time getting to know each other.

That night, as we sat in my dimly lit room, Brian had his arms around me. I said shakily, "I need to be up front with you about everything so you can decide for yourself before we get too far into this."

I proceeded to tell him the details of my past. He held me as I told him about how I'd been abused at thirteen, my toxic marriage, the mistakes I'd made. He listened quietly as I told him of my struggles with food, anxiety, PTSD, and the time I'd desperately wanted to end it all. I shared my insecurities, my grief, and the most vulnerable parts of myself. It was painful and awful, but I needed to lay it all on the line.

When I was finally silent, I watched a single tear fall down his cheek. I reached to wipe it away and held my breath as I waited for him to say something.

"I don't know how you could trust anyone again after that."

His words washed over me and released my tears. He held me as I cried. I had bared my soul and expected he'd want nothing more to do with me, but he met me there in that moment and offered comfort. No guilt, no shame, no judgment. Just acceptance of my pain, my brokenness, all of me. It was as if I were hearing for the first time in my life the words I'd longed to hear when I was thirteen: "It's not your fault."

I knew I wanted him beside me on my path toward healing. I wanted him to be my partner because I knew that we could conquer any obstacle in front of us. I knew he could love me well. While it didn't look at all like what I'd thought I wanted, it was real.

There was freedom in the truth. I felt lighter after revealing myself to him, and our relationship steadily progressed. He was always up for exploring and adventure, and I showed him all of my favorite running spots.

One unseasonably warm Sunday morning in late January, I introduced Brian to one of my favorite trails. It was eight miles round trip. As we returned to the car, we ran along a dirt trail through the trees, jumping over rocks and roots. Brian sped up and started to pull away. Not to be outdone, I sped up as well. A few strides later, I felt a pop in my left hamstring and almost fell to the ground.

"Gah!" I hollered.

Brian came back to where I stood, clutching my leg. "I feel like I just got shot in the back of the leg," I explained.

We walked, hoping I just needed a break. I tried to run again, but it hurt too much. My hamstring was sore, but the real blow was to my pride. I resigned myself to the fact that I had to walk the three miles back to the car, in denial that I was dealing with a serious injury just as my official IRONMAN training was getting underway.

19: TIMING IS EVERYTHING

I called my friend Dr. Laiderman and scheduled an appointment to see him. I'd sent several others to see him for running injuries but never dreamed that I'd need to consult him myself.

Dejectedly, I hobbled into his office, fearing my new dream of becoming an IRONMAN was being snuffed out before training even started. He asked me a bunch of questions about what had happened when the injury occurred, events leading up to it, past injuries, and so on. He had me do squats and watched my form. He determined that my pelvis was twisted, which was creating extra pull on the left side of my body. He did an adjustment and reassured me that he could get me back on track. But running was temporarily out of the picture.

As it turned out, the trauma to my ankle the night before I moved out of my ex-husband's house—the injury I'd chosen to ignore—had come back to bite me. That untreated injury had led to a nagging fatigue in my right hip while I trained for Racine. I'd noticed the hip issue and tried to get by, using a foam roller and other tools to stretch my tight muscles. That had worked temporarily, a Band-Aid fix, until ultimately, my body made it clear that I needed to fix all the problems I'd ignored. Again, I had to get to the root cause of the problem.

As a former IRONMAN himself, Dr. Laiderman was the right doctor for me. He assured me that he'd get me back to running as soon as possible, but he needed to do more work on me before that could happen. We scheduled an appointment for the following week.

Being out of commission for running forced me to do more work on the bike trainer and in the pool. What I could have viewed as a setback actually allowed me time to work on other skills.

A New Opportunity

Sales didn't come naturally to me. At my first Fleet Feet annual review, I learned about metrics. I was shocked to learn that I ranked near the bottom across all three stores. But David and Debby weren't ready to give up on me. They saw something in me I didn't even know was there yet. I persevered, and by the following year, my metrics had completely turned around. I'd improved tremendously and climbed way up the list.

My confidence was at a new high, and I loved my work. I also adored my coworkers and our customers; we shared a passion. I looked for new opportunities to help and took on new responsibilities, such as leading the Thursday night social run.

In addition to providing most of my social life, my job at Fleet Feet involved a lot of fun perks. At staff meetings, we received running gear prizes. We got to wear test products, and I'd occasionally arrive at work to find a new pair of shoes waiting for me. We had staff events where David paid our race entry fees or took us bowling. I couldn't believe my job was so much fun.

The best thing that came out of my first years at Fleet Feet was the relationships I formed. In a new city where I didn't know anyone, I'd built a community of friends who loved and accepted me. They saw me at my best and my worst, but most importantly, they saw me being genuine. I was authentically me as I figured out exactly what that looked like.

Timing was everything. I'd been in communication with one of the managers and had indicated I wanted some variety in my responsibilities. She told me to hang in there and be patient because something was coming.

I got to work one day and logged on to the back-room computer to check my Fleet Feet email. I opened my weekly highlight email and read the part about a new store that would be opening a few miles away, inside the triathlon shop Swim Bike Run.

"Ohhhhhhhh," I said to myself, as it dawned on me. That's why Jaime had been so evasive when I'd prodded her for info. She knew exactly what the plan was for me. My new title of triathlete, among mostly running coworkers, made me the perfect candidate for helping get the new store off the ground.

On February 14, 2014, I helped Kristen open the newest addition to the fleet of stores. I was surrounded by people who could help me figure out the parts of triathlon that were still somewhat foreign to me. It was perfect timing for everyone, especially me.

Tri Bike

Being in the new store provided new challenges, responsibilities, and perks. The bike fitters offered a service that helped customers find a bike that was the right fit, much like I'd done with running shoes. We took turns fitting each other so we could learn the workings of each side of the store.

About a month after I started at the new location, James fitted me for a tri bike. I hadn't planned to buy a bike; my road bike was fine for my IRONMAN, but when I went through the bike-fit process, I fell in love with how good a proper fit on a customized bike felt. It was outfitted with my preferred saddle and aerobars and adjusted to maximize my performance. James offered me a deal I couldn't refuse and allowed me to make payments I could handle.

I named the new bike "Iggy" because she was so fancy. The day I got to take her home with me, I asked my coworker Kerstin to take a photo of me with it.

"You should go outside, and I'll take it in front of the store," Kerstin said.

I stood smiling with my new prize, squinting into the sunlight despite the sunglasses on my face. After that, every shift I worked was a chance to ogle all the fun gadgets I couldn't necessarily afford to add.

I was okay with not being able to purchase everything. I prided myself on getting my training done with the bare essentials. As it was, my super-sleek tri bike seemed way out of my league. In some ways, I felt like an imposter riding it, but I also decided that if I was going to be an IRONMAN, I should start trying to look the part.

20: IT TAKES A VILLAGE

As hesitant as I'd been about social media when I first signed up for Facebook, I learned to love reconnecting with people from my past. Having lived in multiple states growing up, I often wondered if people remembered me. One of my biggest fears was that I was forgettable, and I didn't want that fear to be confirmed. But when I put myself out there, I found that people did remember, and they came out of the woodwork and embraced me.

Growing up in an age of long-distance phone calls and snail mail as the main forms of communication, I'd lost touch with so many friends. But one by one, people came back into my life.

Jayne was the daughter of one of my dad's colleagues. Our families had been fairly close growing up, but she was older than I was. Other than babysitting me occasionally, I didn't think she took much notice of me. Once we hit adulthood though, a few years' age difference didn't seem like much, especially with common experiences to bridge the gap.

Jayne and I were friends on Facebook, and I enjoyed watching her journey. I knew she, too, had been divorced and was rebuilding her life after a destructive marriage. We chatted occasionally, and she encouraged me as I came out of my tragic circumstances and attempted to move forward.

Jayne was dating a triathlete named Jimi who'd competed in several IRONMAN events. Jayne was also a phenomenal endurance athlete, but she preferred to act as Jimi's sherpa on IRONMAN days rather than compete herself.

One morning, I woke up to find a message from her: "Hey, I have a Rudy Project helmet still in the box from last year. It was part of my gear from my team, but I never even used it. If you want it, it's yours. It'll save you some money, and it's a good helmet. Just give me your address, and I'll put it in the mail tomorrow."

I quickly typed, "Wow! That would be amazing, Jayne. I was so not expecting that, but I would seriously appreciate it. Triathlons have really helped me peel back the layers, deal with them, and tell my story. I know you understand where I'm coming from. You've been so supportive of me through everything. I can't thank you enough."

I confirmed that her unused helmet would fit my tiny head and sent her my address. I'd been in desperate need of a new cycling helmet and had wanted to buy one worthy of my new bike, but that was out of my budget with all the other expenses pouring in. I was still using an old, possibly cracked, mountain bike helmet left over from college.

About a week later, a huge box sat on my porch when I arrived home. Wondering why Jayne had used such a gigantic box for a bike helmet, I dragged it through the front door and grabbed the scissors off my desk to cut the tape.

When I opened it, I saw why the box was so big. It was like Christmas! She'd sent not one but two brand new helmets that both matched the black, white, and red of my bike and cycling shoes. She'd included goggles, compression socks, a visor, and other triathlon goodies, along with MSU T-shirts for me and the kids in honor of the Spartans' trip to the NCAA Final Four. As I sat on the floor by my front door, pulling out one thing after another, tears began running down my cheeks.

I was overwhelmed and humbled by her generosity. She'd already given me so much with her encouragement alone, but the box full of surprises was an unexpected and much-appreciated kindness. It reminded me there were people in my corner, rooting me on, helping me succeed.

Summer 2014

The summer months that year were full in every respect. The kids were out of school, and their activities were in full swing. I was working more hours at the new store than I had previously because there were so few of us on staff. I completed two workouts a day as often as I could. And I had a boyfriend I wanted to spend as much time with as possible.

Dr. Laiderman quickly had me back to running, and I continued to see him every week or two for maintenance. After his treatments, running felt so good that my mileage shot back up almost immediately.

In July, a friend from work and I took a weekend trip to Kansas, where I ran my first ultra-marathon. (An ultra consists of any race distance longer than 26.2 miles.) She and I had both led some of the Fleet Feet trail groups, and the Psycho-Wyco 50k was the culmination of the season. After work on a Friday, we hopped in the car and drove across Missouri, carb-loading on Cheeze-Its and Starburst jellybeans. We had every intention of stopping for dinner, but kept driving. By the time we checked into the hotel at 9:30 p.m., we were more tired than hungry.

The next morning started early. We checked out of the hotel, drove to the race site, got our race gear, and prepped for a long, hot day on the trails. We ran three loops on the same ten-mile course through tough, hilly terrain. It felt as if we were running through a rain forest rather than Kansas. The high temp hit almost 100 that afternoon, and the humidity was off the charts. The sun beat down on us when we weren't under the protection of the trees.

The volunteers were fantastic, providing icy, wet towels for our necks and every snack imaginable. As the temperature got hotter, I couldn't get enough of the fresh, cold watermelon they offered. At every aid station, I grabbed a handful of ice and dropped it into my sports bra.

Approximately seven hours after I'd started, I crossed the finish line of my first ultra. There was a reason the motto of the race was "50k the hard way." Once again, I'd pushed my limits and found I could rise to the occasion.

On the drive home, we stopped at a gas station to wash up in the restroom sink and change clothes. We each grabbed a small pizza and devoured it. Then I hurried back home to see Brian, who was waiting for me.

I continued training through the heat of the summer. It wasn't easy, but I found the more cross-training I did, the better athlete I became. With the training, I learned lessons about myself and became a better person in general. Even when my training was at its peak, I could look around and see how much more I enjoyed everything about my life. I was conquering the training instead of it conquering me.

A Tale of Two Centuries

There's a first time for everything. Whether I was ready or not, the time came to ride my first century. As one might expect, a century in the cycling world is one hundred miles.

I'd just completed a grueling half distance triathalon at Border Wars in Alton, Illinois, that I'd used as a training race. It had included a swim in the muddy Mississippi while I was under attack by giant carp, a brutally windy bike ride through the flats of Saint Charles, and then a drastic increase in temperature to eighty-plus degrees on a run course where the race officials ran out of water for the athletes.

I'd chosen Border Wars not for the frills but the convenience and to keep costs low. It was just over the river, so it involved virtually no travel. I wanted another half distance IRONMAN under my belt, and it was a perfect opportunity. It wasn't fast or pretty, but it got the job done and made me a two-time half distance IRONMAN finisher.

Barb, a fellow member of the tri club who was also training for IRONMAN Arizona, had proposed riding a century in nearby Columbia, Illinois. She was a more experienced rider, so I gladly took her up on her offer. After I dropped my kids at school on a Wednesday morning with my bike already loaded on the back of the car, I drove over the river and met Barb in a grocery store parking lot to begin our ride. On this beautiful October day, my mission was to complete my goal of one hundred miles on the bike.

Having just spent a windy day riding fifty-six miles at Border Wars, I wasn't particularly excited about spending the whole day on my bike to almost double that mileage. We planned to stay at an even pace to get it done, not pushing too hard.

I was sure it would be okay, even if it was the tiniest bit grueling. I knew Barb's company, encouragement, and experience would make it tolerable and more enjoyable.

We were wheels down by nine o'clock as planned. I followed along behind Barb as we rode out of the parking lot and onto a country lane. We made a left, rode a couple miles, made a right, and wound around until we were riding on the levee of the river bottom.

The scenery consisted primarily of farmers working in their fields and an occasional combine. We rode and talked, taking in the autumn colors. Barb gave me cycling tips and had me try different techniques every once in a while to see if it increased my pedaling cadence. We talked about our kids and work and a variety of other topics, and the miles passed quickly.

Eventually, we reached the end of the levee and rode on the rolling hills of a two-lane back road. There was a shoulder to ride on, but the semi-trucks flew past at sixty miles per hour, raising my anxiety. When we hit the fifty-mile mark and it was time to turn back, I looked forward to the safe haven of the levee.

Just before we got back to the levee path, we stopped in a little corner store to get more water and supplies and use the restroom; then we got back on the path and kept on pedaling. The sun had shifted from the east side of the sky to the west.

When we hit seventy-five miles, I was at a new personal record for bike distance. I felt stiff and sore through my neck and shoulders, and my feet ached in my cycling shoes. The breeze picked up and the sun beat down, but we kept going.

The miles that had passed quickly on the way out ticked off much more slowly on the way back. Barb pulled ahead, and I struggled to stay behind her. We took a short pit stop and then mounted up for the final stretch. Finally, we turned off the levee and onto the road that led to the parking lot where we'd started.

As we entered the lot, my Garmin beeped at a hundred miles. I did a victory lap and slowed to a stop by my car. Unclipping my feet from the bike pedals, I stopped my Garmin, noting 0.4 miles extra. We'd been riding for six and a half hours.

With Barb's help, I'd completed the task. She was impressed with how well I'd done on my first hundred-miler. She was also impressed that in true Lindsey style, I was still smiling.

School had ended and I needed to pick up my kids, who were still forty minutes away back in Saint Louis. I'd signed them up for the afterschool program that day, not knowing how long the ride would take. I changed into flip-flops and loaded up my gear. I ached, but it was an ache of proud accomplishment. I'd spent the kids' entire school day riding my bike. I'd completed another necessary step toward my goal, and my confidence soared as I drove to pick them up.

A couple weeks later, Steve mentioned he had some vacation days he had to use. I suggested he take a day off work to ride another century with me. I wanted the challenge of more hills. He agreed and mapped a route to meet my requirements. Little did I know what he was planning to throw at me.

Again, I drove the kids to school with my riding gear ready to go, dropped them off, and went directly to Steve's place. I'd teased him so much about being a single guy living in O'Fallon, a family-oriented suburb, that he was finally getting ready to put his place on the market. He gave me a quick tour of the paint job and upgrades he'd been working on, and then we were off.

His planned route didn't let me down. In fact, I quickly regretted telling him to throw in a few hills. We went through Lake Saint Louis to New Melle, on to Innsbrook, Warrenton, and Troy, and then back toward Wentzville. We rode through some beautiful areas and some sketchy spots, and the route was challenging most of the way. He didn't spare me at all.

We stopped for a quick nutrition break, and Steve checked his blood sugar. When we took off again, he said, "Stay on my back tire."

"Oh sure," I said, not feeling at all confident that I'd be able to comply.

I pedaled my heart out, but it was only a matter of seconds until he pulled away. It wasn't long at all until he was far in the distance.

We came to a stop again several miles down the road, and he chided me, "That was staying on my back tire?"

He pushed me, but he also took care of me and waited for me to catch up. When we finally stopped at a fast-food restaurant in Troy to use the restroom and take a little break. I wanted desperately to be done. I joked about calling his mom to pick me up. We were a little more than halfway, and I was feeling every bit of it. The hills were kicking my butt, and I wanted to quit, but I knew quitting would feel worse than the physical pain and exhaustion.

"Okay, let's get this over with," I said as we clipped back in. By the time we wound our way back to Lake Saint Louis, my fatigue had given way to crabbiness.

"Get on the sidewalk!" the driver of a pickup yelled out his window.

"I'm not allowed on the sidewalk!" I yelled back.

I fumed at the rudeness of drivers, but that helped fuel me along. We hit one hundred miles, and with quite a way to go to get back to Steve's place. I wanted to dismount my bike and chuck it off an overpass. I hurt, and my physical energy was gone. I was running on pure will and determination, but even that was waning.

I kept Steve in sight and told myself we were almost there. Each turn brought the hope we were done, but we kept going. Finally, his neighborhood came into view, then his condo, and at last, my car.

I disengaged from my pedals, glided to a stop, then leaned my bike against my car and promptly lay down in the grass. I was ecstatic to be done with that soul-crushing experience.

Steve lay down next to me, and it wasn't long before he had me laughing. I'd completed another century, longer and even more difficult than the first. I continued to push my limits, and, in doing so, I was proving to myself that limits were merely an illusion.

Going the Distance

Training for an event of IRONMAN Arizona's magnitude involved a lot of grunt work. It meant fitting in workouts early in the morning, late at night, or whenever I could. There were a lot of miles on the bike or the trails and a lot of laps in the pool. It wasn't glamorous.

Timing continued to be everything. Not long after I'd registered for IRONMAN Arizona, a new Gold's Gym opened up down the road from my house, even closer than the gym I'd previously been humiliated out of. There was rarely anyone in the pool at the times I swam, so it was like scoring my own private pool. I spent a fair amount of time staring at the blue line on the bottom while counting laps.

As I juggled my retail schedule and my time with my kids, I was rarely able to join any group workouts. I completed a lot of my mileage solo, which provided solitude and allowed me time to process my thoughts away from all the activity usually going on around me. But occasionally, a perfectly timed opportunity for company presented itself.

I knew that pool swimming could take me only so far. I needed to log more time in open water, so when Luis, who lived at Lake Saint Louis, offered up a Sunday morning swim to attempt the full IRONMAN distance of 2.4 miles, I knew I couldn't pass it up.

We set a date for our practice swim and invited Steve to join us. Luis had measured the course and made our game plan. It was late October, so the water temp would be on the cool side. That meant a full-sleeve wetsuit, which terrified me, as the few times I'd used it, I'd felt choked and suffocated, leading to panic attacks in the water. But I had to get used to it for longer distances in case I needed it on the big day. Besides, the cool water temp was still warmer than the air on that chilly fall morning.

I arrived in the parking lot before Luis and Steve, even though I had the longest drive to get there. I wasn't mentally prepared to get suited up yet, so I sat in the car, enjoying the comfortable warmth for as long as possible.

I shot off a text to Teri: "I'm scared of this swim, so I'm drawing strength from you. Trying to be courageous."

"You can do this," she texted. "I know you can."

"Here goes nothing," I shot back.

At that moment, Steve's car pulled in next to mine. I looked over to see him flash his big smile my direction. I knew my nerves showed on my face.

He got out of the car and immediately started getting ready, easily sliding into his wetsuit and gathering his towel, goggles, and swim cap.

I slowly joined him and stuck my hands in the pocket of my hoodie as I looked at him, I whined, "I don't wanna."

He continued smiling at me, and soon he was laughing as I began the awkward dance of getting into my wetsuit.

Luis arrived shortly thereafter, chipper as ever. The two happy guys were determined to get me through what loomed ahead of me, come hell or high water.

We made our way down to the beach and left our gear in a pile. We pulled on swim caps, defogged our goggles, and Luis took a quick video as we checked the temperature of the water. The weather was chilly; we could see our breath in the crisp air.

The swim was going to take a long time, and it was going to challenge me. I knew I couldn't procrastinate any longer, because I needed time to drive to the store, shower, and clock in for my shift afterward.

"You can do this, Lindsey," Luis said confidently as we waded farther into the water. "Steve, stay close to her to give her a sense of comfort and direction. I'll swim up ahead to clear any debris."

I took a deep breath and submerged my body in the water, absorbing the shock to my system. It took a few minutes for the wetsuit to adjust and provide insulation for my body.

We began our slow, tedious procession through the water and headed straight toward the rocks on the other side. In a few minutes, my wetsuit loosened up and felt slightly less restrictive.

After a few hundred meters, I popped my head up, and my body bobbed as I treaded water.

"You okay?" Steve asked.

"Yeah, just needed to catch my breath for a sec," I answered.

"Keep on going, Lindsey!" Luis yelled from up ahead.

We continued on our course. Stroke, stroke, stroke, breathe. Stroke, stroke, stroke, breathe. Sometimes I pushed myself to four, five, even six strokes between breaths. I was comfortable breathing on either side, so I kept swimming and remembered Andy's words, "Breathe when you need to." I fell into a rhythm, and the boys checked on me periodically. I practiced sighting Luis up ahead of me to keep track of where I was going, so I could swim the most direct route.

We kept swimming through the dark, murky water. When we got to the rocks, we turned and had a long straight shot to the farthest point. The course Luis had plotted was essentially a large, abstract triangle we had to complete twice. Red and yellow leaves rained down on us intermittently from the trees surrounding the lake.

We completed the first loop in about an hour, took a short break, and went right back in. After what felt like days, we made the final turn back toward the beach. By that time, I felt reasonably comfortable in the water. I'd made peace with the wetsuit, but I was tired and ready for our swim to be over. I wasn't doing as well at monitoring my direction. At one point, I nearly swam straight into a dock. Even in my exhaustion, I felt a force pulling me back to shore.

Finally, the beach came into view. As I checked my sight, I saw Luis's kids jumping up and down on the sand, cheering us on, cheering me on. I kept swimming, stroke after stroke, and then my feet touched the sand.

I carefully lifted myself out of the water. Luis took a video to capture the moment. I pulled my goggles off as Steve stood by smiling and gave me a high five. They both hugged me in congratulations, and I shakily made my way onto the beach with Steve and Luis on either side of me.

We checked our Garmins. We'd gone the full 2.4 miles in just over two hours. That was twenty minutes less than the time allotted to complete the first phase of an IRONMAN. I knew without a doubt I could do the full swim fast enough.

So many emotions flooded me at once: I was elated, exhausted, relieved, and bewildered. Luis's daughter Adrianna danced happily around, excitedly celebrating my accomplishment.

This child who barely knew me was acting as I felt but was too depleted to articulate.

Luis's wife, Melissa, had prepared and brought a huge breakfast to the beach for us. She laid out a spread on the picnic table with all kinds of options. I was drooling as I stripped the wetsuit off my arms, pulled it down to my waist, and wrapped a towel around my shoulders to stay warm. I was too weak to stand but too excited to sit, so I put one knee on the bench and leaned on the table.

"What can I get you?" Melissa asked. She proceeded to load a plate for me with egg casserole and cinnamon rolls per my request. Then she handed me a Styrofoam cup of orange juice and another with hot chocolate.

I gulped down the juice quickly to get some calories back in my body, popped a bite of roll into my mouth, and stabbed some eggs with a plastic fork. I hurriedly ate my plate of food knowing that work was beckoning. I wanted to eat more, but I had to get going.

I thanked my friends for everything, and they congratulated me again. I was beaming. I'd done what I needed to, and my confidence rose to a new level. I left them still celebrating my victory on the little beach.

I walked up the hill and back to my car, turned on the ignition, and cranked the heat up before I finished removing my wetsuit and put it in the back of the car. I slipped my flip-flops back on and slid into the seat in my damp swimsuit, towel, and hoodie.

Before pulling out of the parking lot, I pulled out my phone and, with happy tears rolling down my cheeks, sent Teri another text: I did it. :) When I arrived at the store thirty minutes later, I saw Teri's response: "Of course you did."

21: ON MY WAY

With only a few weeks until IRONMAN Arizona, I found myself with some extra time on my hands. As race day approached, we entered into what athletes refer to as "the taper." We tapered off on our training for a few weeks to give our bodies more rest in anticipation of the greater task ahead of us.

One such day, I received a text from Teri: "What are you doing? Are you free this afternoon? I have a favor. Give me a call."

Fortunately, I wasn't busy. I'd been planning to do a short run at some point before picking up my kids from school, but I stopped whatever menial task I was doing and called Teri.

"Hey," she said. "I have a friend who's a reporter for one of the local news stations. She's doing a story about triathlons, and she asked me to find her an athlete. Is it okay if I give her your number?"

"Um, yes!" I said. "Of course!"

"Great! I think she wants to try to interview you this afternoon, maybe running or riding or something. Are you available?"

"I sure am!"

"Okay, her name is Farah. She's probably going to call you in a little while."

We hung up, and my phone rang again a few minutes later.

"Hi, Lindsey. This is Farah. I hope it's okay that Teri shared your info with me. I need some help."

"Sure, no problem," I said.

She explained that she needed to interview someone training for a big race. She'd contacted Teri, who knows everyone in Saint Louis who's training for everything. She was hoping to meet me at Forest Park or one of the other local hot spots for training and wondered how soon I could be there. I explained that I was at home and I just needed to change quickly, so I could meet her in about forty-five minutes.

We decided to meet at Creve Coeur Lake, a better halfway point for us, to save time. I changed into running tights and a Fleet Feet tank top. I figured if I was going to be on TV, I wanted to represent the brand. I threw together my cycling gear just in case, tossed everything in the car, put my bike on the rack and a banana in my mouth, and headed for Sailboat Cove.

When I got there, I easily spotted Farah in the station vehicle with a cameraman already prepping. I parked and jumped out of the car with a huge smile on my face. We introduced ourselves, and she thanked me for being available.

Farah asked me a series of questions about myself about my upcoming race and my training. They filmed me as I jogged along the path next to the lake.

The interview took less than thirty minutes. Farah was so fun to talk to, I enjoyed every second of feeling a little like a celebrity-in-the-making.

We parted ways, and I headed home to get ready to pick up my kids from school. I sent out a heads-up to my running and triathlon friends in the community to look for me on the nightly news.

When the kids got into the car later that afternoon, I said, "Hey, guess what? I got interviewed today, and I'm going to be on the news tonight."

We were all excited as we huddled around the TV to watch the segment. The story was really about the possibility of bringing an IRONMAN event to Saint Louis. My interview was designed to give the story a warm, fuzzy feel. As the featured athlete, I was front and center on the screen, talking about triathlon. The segment showed me running along the path, and I heard my own voice describing what made running and triathlon so special to me. Farah made me sound like a superhero as a working single mom training for such a big race.

The segment ended with Farah saying, "In just two weeks, Lindsey Jacobs is on her way to becoming an IRONMAN in Arizona."

My phone started blowing up from all the people who saw me. I had a lump in my throat, tears in my eyes, and I couldn't wipe the smile off my face.

22: IRONMAN ARIZONA 2014

When I started the journey to IRONMAN, it was about getting to the finish line. By the time we headed to Arizona, I knew it was about so much more than that. On Wednesday morning, November 12, 2014, I drove my boys to school and said goodbye to them for a week. Then I went home to finish preparing for a cross-country road trip.

The tree in my front yard, always the last tree on the street to change color and shed its leaves, was brilliantly ablaze in red and orange. I paused to take in its majesty as I packed my swim and bike gear into the back of the car. I knew we'd likely return the following week to bare branches. I pondered other changes that would take place over the next week.

My daughter, Ally, was upstairs in her room getting packed. I'd worked it out with her dad to allow her to come with us for the week. When Dan and my boyfriend, Brian, arrived, we loaded their bags into the SUV. Then we locked the bikes onto the back and set out for warmer weather. Dan drove the first shift, with Brian riding shotgun, and Ally and I hunkered down in the backseat, settled in for the time being.

The miles passed; the sun rose high in the sky and then faded into the horizon. It was dark when we stopped in Amarillo for dinner at Cracker Barrel, and it was snowing. I took the late shift driving into the darkness of New Mexico. When we stopped in Albuquerque to fill up the gas tank, the temperature was hovering in single digits. I didn't have a coat, so I wrapped up in a blanket.

I drove until I couldn't keep my eyes open any longer. Dan took over and put the pedal to the metal while I curled up in the backseat with Ally to take a nap.

When I awoke a couple hours later, the guys informed me that we were on course to make it to the south rim of the Grand Canyon in time for sunrise. As we pulled into the parking lot, we stared out the window. It was just starting to get light out, and a herd of elk meandered on the road.

"Oh, look over there. There's a bunch of them!" We were fascinated by the big animals so close to us.

"I still can't believe you got us here for this," I exclaimed.

"You don't even want to know how fast I drove," Dan responded.

"No, I don't," I said, as I raised my eyebrows to Ally.

We pulled into one of the many empty spots in the lot and were surprised by the spectacle of two elk sparring. Dan intentionally picked a spot far enough away from them so we were safe to get out of the car, but close enough we could watch. The night sky was giving way to dawn, and we wanted to be on the edge of the canyon for the view.

We walked out to the rim, taking in the vastness of the canyon as we waited for the sun to fully appear. The breeze was chilly, so we wrapped blankets around ourselves and huddled together to try to stay warm. As I stood surrounded by my love, my little girl, and one of my best friends, I watched the sun poke through the clouds over the edge of a natural wonder. I could have stayed in that moment forever, but we still had work to do.

We ambled back to the car, grateful for its warmth, and began the final stretch of the drive south into Tempe. The redrock scenery was stunning, and the temperature outside began to rise. We ditched our hoodies, exchanged shoes for flip-flops, and rolled the windows down to feel the fresh air on our wind-burnt cheeks.

We cruised into the Phoenix metropolitan area in early afternoon and pulled up to the townhouse we'd rented with a group of friends for the week. Some of our housemates were from the group I'd volunteered with at IRONMAN Arizona the previous year. Farrell was staying at her aunt and uncle's house again with her husband and her mom. Adrienne had flown in; the others weren't there yet. Kelly and Sheila were going to join us, and Allison, a late addition to the group, was taking the couch.

We unloaded the bikes, tri gear, and bags and claimed our rooms. Shortly after that, Adrienne pulled her rental car into the driveway, glad to see her bike had made it in one piece.

"We almost had to sacrifice it to an elk," we joked and filled her in on our adventure.

After unpacking and getting organized, Adrienne and I headed to the grocery store. As triathletes, we needed to load up on carbohydrates, so food was a priority.

We brought the bags of food into the kitchen, filled the fridge, and then made our way to IRONMAN Village in the heart of downtown Tempe.

We met up with Farrell so we could all attend the athlete meeting and race check-in together. We listened to the announcer give various information and instructions about the ins and outs of the race. I took it in as well as I could, but it felt somewhat overwhelming.

We walked to the check-in table.

"What's your name?" the volunteer asked.

"Lindsey Jacobs," I answered.

He checked my ID, found me on the list, and wrote my number on a brightly colored swim cap. Then he securely fastened a plastic bracelet to my wrist, bearing my athlete number: 1241. It was exhilarating, terrifying, and surreal. I was actually going to attempt something I'd at one time thought impossible.

We wandered through the IRONMAN apparel tent, carefully selecting mementos and treasures to forever serve as reminders of IRONMAN Arizona 2014. I picked out a sweatshirt and a coffee mug, being conservative because I didn't know what the outcome would be. I hoped to return the day after the race to peruse the finishers' gear that wasn't available prior to the race.

With so much to do to prepare and the race still a few days away, I held my nerves at bay with activities like eating lunch outside, easy practice workouts, and packing gear bags. My mom, my niece, my brother and his new wife, and my brand-new nephew arrived from southern California. Ally and I were excited to meet little Quincy, who was only a few months old.

Ally left the townhouse that had become IRONMAN Central and went to spend the next few days with my family.

They did their own visit to the Grand Canyon, swam in the pool, and allowed me space to get ready for what I'd come to do.

Gearing Up

The day before IRONMAN Arizona, Adrienne and I went to the course to drop off our bikes and meet Farrell for a pre-race warm-up. We hauled our gear around, jumped into Tempe Town Lake for a swim, and did a short run along the waterfront. Saying goodbye to our carefully packed transition bags with everything we needed to go from one discipline to the next, we dropped them in the transition areas.

We went back to the house and cleaned up; then, I left to have lunch with Casey, a dear friend from high school who'd since moved to Arizona.

I arrived at Bar Louie and recognized her immediately. "It's so good to see you!" we gushed as we hugged each other after so many years.

We claimed a table outside and ordered snacks, chatting easily. We talked about our struggles and joys, catching up on the twenty years since high school.

"I can't believe you're doing an IRONMAN!" she said. "Actually, I can." She was beyond proud of my accomplishments, but I still had a big one ahead of me.

That evening, Brian, Dan, and I met up with my family for an early dinner in Scottsdale. I'd chosen Buca di Beppo because they seat people and serve family style. I sat at a large table, surrounded by people I loved, eating delicious food, and soaking in the beauty of the moment. After dinner, we wandered down the street and found an ice cream shop for dessert.

As we parted ways for the night, sharing hugs and well wishes, we knew we'd see each other on the course the next day. It was bittersweet saying goodnight to the people who loved me most in the world. I was grateful beyond words that they'd come to support me in my venture, but I deeply felt my dad's absence.

When we got back to the house, everyone settled in for the evening. Only a few of us were competing the next day, but everyone was involved somehow. Kelly, Adrienne, and I were on the verge of attempting a full distance IRONMAN. Dan and Allison were volunteering. Brian and Kelly's wife, Sheila, were our support crew.

Our nerves were running high by this point, but so was the encouragement from friends. Texts and Facebook messages poured in from people sending good luck and best wishes. I was overwhelmed and overjoyed to see how many people were cheering me on from all across the country.

We set out bananas, bottled water, and various other items for the morning. I brought my tri-tats, temporary tattoos with official numbers that triathletes wear on their bodies, to the kitchen for Allison to help me arrange the numbers on my arms. On the second number, she forgot to peel the plastic backing off, so instead of transferring to my skin, it transferred to the piece of plastic, leaving a gap where the number 2 should have been on my right arm.

I collapsed in a fit of giggles, to which Allison said, "I'm so glad I did this to you and not to someone who'd care and be really mad at me." We laughed until our stomachs hurt, and my heart was happy to know she saw me as someone who didn't get so caught up in the minutia that I couldn't find the humor and joy in any situation.

Then it was time to calm down and try to sleep. I don't know how, with the excitement and anticipation swirling around me, but somehow, I fell asleep, for a few hours at least.

Race Day Arrival

At four in the morning, while it was still pitch dark outside, it was time to get moving. I'd never been much of a morning person, never caring to get up at any time that didn't at least have a six in front of it. But for some reason, on race days, the alarm would immediately pull me from a foggy haze and push me into beast mode.

I popped right up and tried to make as little noise as possible, knowing others were still sleeping. I was in the middle of my morning routine, brushing my teeth and braiding my hair, when a loud crash broke the morning stillness. I learned later that Dan, in an effort to not wake anyone, had tried to tiptoe down the stairs without turning the lights on but, instead, had fallen down the stairs. He broke several toes in the process, but duty called, and he reported to his volunteer station on the swim course.

I made my way to the kitchen in my sweats. Neither Adrienne nor I felt like talking. We drank coffee, tried to eat breakfast, and filled our water bottles to add to our waiting bikes. We attempted to keep things light, but the air was thick with nervousness about the challenge that loomed before us. As rookies, we were uncertain of what lay ahead that Sunday, but we both kept taking one little step after another, side by side.

In the chilly pre-dawn air, we tossed our swim gear into the SUV and silently stared out the windows as Brian drove us to the course and dropped us off. He went to park the car as we set about, stuffing last-minute items into transition bags and checking on our bikes, to which we attached water bottles and necessary nutrition items.

When I'd picked up my race packet the first day, I'd been given a green swim cap marked with #1241. I'd failed to realize at the time that I should have received a pink cap. We set off to find a volunteer table to exchange my cap. They wrote out my number on a pink cap and told me to keep the green as a souvenir.

They said it wouldn't have mattered, but I wanted to make sure I did everything precisely so there wouldn't be any reason to be kicked off the race course. I knew I'd already be racing the clock to get from one event to the next in the allotted time before the transition cutoffs. I was fairly sure I could make up some time during the run, but I had a limited amount of time to get to each transition point.

If I didn't make it in time, I'd be disqualified, not allowed to continue, and marked with my first ever DNF—"did not finish." I didn't want to think of that as an option, but realistically, if something went wrong, like a bad swim or a flat tire on the bike, it was a possibility, and it hung in my mind.

Adrienne didn't have tri-tats like mine, so she needed to get body-marked. We found the volunteers with the permanent markers writing numbers on the athletes' arms and calves. My numbers were mostly complete from the tri-tats Allison had successfully adhered to my body, but I had our volunteer fill in the gap of the missing 2 from the night before. I laughed nervously as I explained to the volunteer what had happened.

When we'd checked everything off the to-do list, we got in the line for one last attempt at the Port-O-Potty before putting on our wetsuits. While we awaited our turn, Ron came by. He was also a first-timer who'd been with us to volunteer and register the year before. His friend Mark had, unfortunately, sustained an injury and was unable to compete with us.

"Hey, Ron," Adrienne greeted him. "How's it going?"

"I'm pretty nervous," Ron answered.

"I'm staying away from the word *nervous*," I explained. "I prefer *anxious*, because I know I'll be better once we get this thing underway. Waiting around is kind of torturous though."

We gave each other last-minute reminders to enjoy the day and trust the training we'd done to get there. After Ron left and we stood there among thousands of athletes, volunteers, and spectators, I looked at Adrienne and said, "I'm so glad we're doing this together." I couldn't imagine trying to navigate the chaos and uncertainty on my own. Even though we were both newbies, it was comforting to be together.

After our turn in the Port-O-Potty, it was time to begin the daunting task of putting on wetsuits. It was still dark outside, and the temperature had risen only to fifty-seven degrees. As I stripped off my sweatpants and hoodie and wore only my faded, stretched-out swimsuit, pure adrenaline kept me from noticing the cool air that brushed my skin. If I had goosebumps, they were due to the anticipation of what I was about to embark on.

I struggled and fought with my wetsuit to get it in place. People had suggested various products, like Body Glide, but they'd never made it any easier for me. As I jumped up and down, wondering if I looked as foolish as I felt trying to get the rubber legs in place, I caught sight of Brian up on a hill watching us. He raised his hand in a wave; I blew him a kiss and continued the process. Finally, I pulled up the wetsuit enough to put my arms through the armholes. I'd opted for my sleeveless wetsuit despite the water temp indicating that sleeves would probably have been the better choice. I hadn't been one to go with the majority at any of my races to date, so why would I start with this one? As athletes, we all usually adhere to the superstition of "Nothing new on race day."

Adrienne and I left our bikes in the transition area, dropped off our gear bags and went to line up with the mass of other swimmers ready to get things underway. I turned and gave Brian one last wave. We knew each other well enough that I could tell he was feeling all the nerves I felt.

Adrienne and I walked toward the start of IRONMAN Arizona 2014. It felt utterly unreal.

23: LAYING IT ALL ON THE LINE

IRONMAN Arizona 2014 was one of the last IRONMAN events to do a mass start, which meant we'd all go to the start line in the water and begin at the same time when the cannon went off. At that point, the clock would start ticking, and I'd have two hours and twenty minutes to get through the 2.4-mile swim course and out of the water.

People were already in the lake treading water or warming up. Some of the lucky ones had gotten in early enough to claim a spot on the ledge built into the man-made lake wall near the start. I wanted to be near the back of the swimmers to avoid faster swimmers climbing over me but not too far away from the start line. I also wanted to give my body time to adjust to the water, but I didn't want to waste energy treading water for very long. It was a strategic balance of timing and placement, and I questioned whether I was doing it right.

As we mixed into the herd of swimmers corralled between the water's edge and a sea of spectators, we found a couple other Saint Louis athletes who filtered into the line with us. Melissa and Tracy were also first-timers, and it was comforting to know that among all the athletes, several were in the same novice position I was.

We put on our matching pink IRONMAN Arizona swim caps as we neared the swim entry. Thoughts of "I don't want to do this. I don't want to get in the water" started to repeat on a loop in my mind.

At the precise moment I felt tears start to well up in my eyes, I caught sight of a large neon sign. Just as I realized the sign had my name on it, I noticed my brother waving at me. Amazingly, he recognized me amidst the hundreds of athletes all in wetsuits and swim caps.

As the line edged closer, I leaned over the make-shift orange fence and stole a quick hug from my mom and my brother AJ. I adjusted my goggles as I recalled seeing my dad's face in the sea of people at my first marathon years before. It was enough to remind me that I could do the hard thing that was in front of me, and not only that, but I wanted to do it.

The next thing I knew, I was on the platform, green turf prickling my bare feet, and then carefully making my way down the stairs into the lake. Volunteers surrounded me, assisting by grabbing arms and hands, trying to keep things efficient and orderly as all the swimmers entered the water.

There was no time to worry about how the water would feel. I didn't think; I just leapt in. The cold water was a shock, but with the large number of swimmers behind me, I got out of the way as quickly as I could, still trying to keep an eye on Adrienne. It wasn't long before my wetsuit did what it was designed to do and insulated my body from the cold, except my bare feet, arms, and face.

Several yards out from the stairs, Adrienne and I regrouped and stayed together as we swam toward the bridge that marked the starting area. We knew we had only another minute or two until the cannon would signal the beginning of our all-day adventure.

We bobbed in the water, with the sun just starting to show itself. Adrienne asked if she could say a quick prayer for us. I wholeheartedly agreed, and under a bridge, while cycling our legs in the water to stay upright, Adrienne prayed.

"Lord, I ask for safety and protection for all the athletes here today. Thank you for the opportunity you've given us to be here, and please give us strength for the journey in front of us. Amen."

"Amen," I echoed.

I gave my gear one last check, and less than a minute later, the gun went off. I pushed the start button on my Garmin, and we were on our way. Adrienne and I separated almost instantly. While I hoped I would see her again somewhere during the day, I knew that was highly unlikely.

Within seconds, I was fully aware it was going to be an even more challenging swim than I'd considered, which was saying something, since I thought I'd considered every possible thing that could happen. Despite my attempt to place myself away from as many swimmers as I could, I was surrounded by bodies, all with the same goal in mind: Make it out to the turnaround and back to the swim exit stairs as quickly as possible.

It resembled water boxing more than swimming. Not only that, but my goggles, which had been fine the previous day at the practice swim, began leaking immediately. I kept stopping to readjust them, no small effort in the midst of a bunch of people who seemed to be trying to drown me. I knew I didn't have time to waste, so I tried to keep swimming with my right eye closed, as that was the side that kept filling with water.

About a hundred meters in, my focus on my goggles shifted when I felt a sharp pain to my face. I didn't know if it was an elbow or a foot, but someone's flailing body part knocked me hard. Shocked and disoriented, I popped my face out of the water. My nose was bleeding, and my lip was already swollen.

I wondered for about half a second what I should do. I glanced around looking for a volunteer on a kayak so I could grab hold temporarily to get my bearings, but none were near enough. I determined I didn't have much choice other than to keep swimming.

As I swam, I lamented the fact that my goggles were leaking, the sun was blinding me when I tried to sight the next buoy, and I would have a fat, swollen lip in all the photos of the day. As I continued on, I realized that the cold water was acting as an anti-inflammatory, effectively reducing the swelling. My nose didn't seem to be bleeding any longer, but I wasn't going to stop to find out.

I kept swimming, and my goggles continued to leak. Eventually, I started throwing elbows to protect myself from the bodies nearby. At one point, it felt as if someone was trying to pull my wetsuit off my body as he swam over the top me. I wanted to yell at him, "Get off of me!" but with my face in the water, I couldn't yell. Again, I just kept swimming.

I fought the water in my goggles and the glare of the sun, but I was getting close to the buoy marking the mile turnaround. As I made the turn, I stole a quick glance at my watch. It said forty-six minutes. For me, that was a record, and I felt a little more confident that I would make the 2:20 swim cutoff.

But just as my confidence started to rise, so did the wind. I felt waves, as if motorboats were racing past, producing a big wake for us to contend with. As I looked up to sight my next buoy, I was certain there were no boats other than the kayakers. I knew Dan was in one of them, and I kept wishing he'd spot me and yell my name loud enough for me to hear. The wind kicked up another notch, and the waves grew more fierce.

"Not again," I thought to myself. I didn't want to fight waves again, but I had no choice. I knew I had to keep taking one stroke after another, even when it felt as if I were making no forward progress at all. I went from one buoy to the next, and then on to the next one, slowly but steadily. I heard my swim coach, Andy, in my mind, reminding me to keep my elbows up, fingertips pointed down, and breathe when I needed to.

As I swam back under the bridge, I wondered if anyone I knew was up there among the spectators and if so, could they recognize me. I only had one final push left to get back to the stairs. Just a few more breaths, just a few more strokes.

I grabbed hold of the steps and, with the help of a volunteer, carefully eased my wobbly body up and out of the water. As I stood to climb the stairs, my legs were shaky, and I felt dizzy. I grabbed the railing and staggered from one volunteer to the next until I reached the top of the steps. I pulled my goggles off my face, and without being able to see myself, I knew I had red rings around my puffy eyes.

Next, I stumbled toward the wetsuit strippers as I unzipped and pulled my arms through, lowering the wetsuit down past my hips. I found someone to assist me and sat down on the ground so he could pull it off from the bottom. As he pulled, he lifted me off the ground, and the process seemed to take longer than it should have. After he helped me to my feet and handed my wetsuit back to me, someone else wrapped a mylar blanket around my shoulders and pointed me in the direction of T1.

I jogged with my wetsuit tucked under one arm, using the other hand to hold the wrap around myself. As I hurried, I looked down at my watch. I didn't fully register what I saw, but I knew it was around 1:40. One hour and forty-two minutes? Forty-eight minutes? I wasn't sure, but it didn't matter. Even though it had taken me a full hour to complete the second half of the swim, I'd still finished well under the time limit. I'd accomplished the first leg of an IRONMAN, completing the discipline that had plagued me the most, with time to spare.

The transition tent seemed a mile from the swim exit. My brain was water-logged and foggy, and my freezing, bare feet were covered with sand and grass. The air temp in the low sixties felt even colder on my bare, wet skin. I kept willing my body to move forward toward my bag with my dry cycling clothes inside.

As I ran through the snaking make-shift fences guiding me into T1, I passed Brian. I'm sure there were probably other people nearby, but in my memory, he was there by himself, grinning at me like a beacon telling to keep going. I don't recall what, if anything, I said to him or if he said anything to me. Just knowing he was there was enough for me.

I shivered as I searched through an ocean of identical plastic bags designated by athlete number. I spotted my bag, grabbed it, and ran into the big white tent with more volunteers standing by to assist.

Embrace the Suck

Dropping all my gear before me, I sat down on a metal folding chair. A woman appeared in front of me, at the ready, asking how she could help. I wanted to get dry, so she opened my bag and pulled out my Malibu Marathon beach towel, which I wrapped around myself as I stripped off my swimsuit.

She pulled out my cycling shorts and my sports bra and helped me put them on. Meanwhile, another volunteer poured warm water on my feet to get the grass and debris off my skin before I put on socks and cycling shoes.

I dressed in the red and orange tri top Sally had given me so I could represent both Fleet Feet and Swim Bike Run. I shoved Huma Gels into the back pockets of my bike jersey to give me a much-needed energy boost. The lady helping me asked what else she could do. I managed to request sunscreen through chattering teeth, so she sprayed my arms and shoulders as I clicked the latch of my bike helmet under my chin.

She pulled my new rimless Tifosi sunglasses out of the case and handed them to me, then stuffed the rest of my gear back into the plastic bag. I don't know if I ever thanked the women who assisted me, but, telepathically, I kept repeating those words over and over as they tended to my needs.

I emerged from the tent, and the warm sun felt good on my skin. I put my sunglasses on as I ran through the racks of bikes. I was surprised by how many bikes were still there, fully expecting mine to be the only one left. I yelled out my race number, and a volunteer pulled my bike off the rack and brought it to me near the huge inflatable arch marked "Bike Out."

When I got across the mount line, where I was allowed to get on my bike, I clipped in and set off on a 112-mile bike ride through the desert. My brain was still reeling from everything that had already taken place that morning, so I tried to calm my mind and settle in for a long afternoon in the saddle. The course was a loop of approximately thirty-five miles we'd complete three times.

Chip at Swim Bike Run had warned me before I left, "No matter what anyone tells you, the Arizona bike course is not flat, so be prepared for hills, and keep your legs going on the way down so they don't cramp up." I took his word for it, and I was ready to eat some hills.

However, I hadn't eaten anything since the Sports Beans I'd munched on while making my way to the swim start, so getting a jump on nutrition was key. I needed some calories, stat! I reached into the bento box mounted to the handlebars of my bike and grabbed a piece of the peanut butter and jelly Bonk Breaker bar

I'd cut up that morning. I popped a piece in my mouth every few miles, a tip I'd borrowed from Barb after our century ride.

The first loop was exciting. As we headed away from IRONMAN Village and out of downtown Tempe, I quickly arrived at the spot where the Swim Bike Run cheering squad had planned to gather, and I flashed a big smile as I sped past orange-clad Renee, Allison, Barb's husband Greg, and several others. Their encouragement was the boost I needed to send me up the hill.

The scenery was beautiful, and as the incline increased, I saw the pros and the elites speeding by in the opposite direction. I kept my eyes peeled for familiar faces or, more aptly, familiar bikes.

The road became steeper, and the wind picked up again. I tried to remember which aid station Ken said he'd be working, and I scanned the faces of the volunteers holding out water bottles and bananas for us to grab as we rode by. I never saw him, but it was a helpful distraction to keep looking.

Dropping into low gear, I headed up a hill, thinking to myself, "Surely, this is the steepest part," but the next hill proved me wrong. At the same time, the wind gusted. I feared falling over, but somehow I kept going.. Occasionally, I wondered if I could walk up the hill faster than I could pedal. At other times, the wind would come from a different angle, causing me to swerve and overcorrect. To anyone who didn't know better, I might have appeared to be riding under the influence. Fortunately, everyone else on the course was dealing with the same issues.

I kept hoping the turnaround was at the top of the next hill, but this leg seemed never ending. I started to wonder how I was going to do the whole loop again, not just once but two more times. Finally, I came to the turnaround. I'd checked off only about seventeen miles, but it felt like fifty.

I dismounted and parked my bike in a rack, allowing myself a few minutes at the aid station to use the Port-O-Potty and take a short break. Even though my bike had been custom fit to me, being on it for hours at a time took a toll.

I grabbed a handful of pretzels from a big plastic container on a table and shoved a couple in my mouth, then got back on and headed down the hill. I remembered what Chip had said about the course not being flat and used my legs on the way back down so they didn't tighten up. Despite my fear of going too fast and crashing, I used the downhill and the tail wind to my advantage as much as could.

It was good to see the Swim Bike Run cheerleaders right where they said they'd stay. I learned later that they were glad to see each of us pass by and know we were okay, as they'd heard reports of harsh winds and several crashes. By this point, my motto of the day had become "Embrace the suck," especially since I knew it was going to suck more before it got better.

As hard as the first time up the mountain had been, the second climb was worse. It wasn't new territory anymore, and I knew I had to conquer it again. The wind blew harder, the hills grew steeper, and the pain increased. I saw cacti bending in the wind and tumbleweeds blow by.

I kept repeating the words "Just keep going, just keep going, just keep going" over and over in my head. It never occurred to me to give up, but when it got really hard, I wanted it to be over. Then I remembered how much hard stuff I'd already made it through and kept pedaling with even more determination.

The cyclists on the course had thinned out on the second loop, but there were still a lot of people. I'd pass someone, and immediately, someone else would pass me. I didn't talk to anyone; I focused on breathing, put my head down, and pedaled.

We were competing with each other, but more than that, we were each competing with ourselves. A bright shining sense of unspoken camaraderie lighting our way to the same end goal. I continued to scan the faces along the sidelines, but no Ken. I scanned the cyclists and thought I saw Adrienne with the bright pink tape on her knee, but I wasn't convinced it wasn't a hallucination.

Arriving at the turnaround again, I allowed myself another pit stop. I ate some more pretzels, sprayed on more sunscreen, and shoved some Vaseline in my cycling shorts to ease the chafing that had set in. With all that swimming, cycling, and sweating, there really was no way to avoid it—ouch! Then I got back on the bike and kept going.

I rode down the hill, looking forward to arriving at Bike Special Needs where each athlete had put together a small bag of items they might want mid-bike. I wanted my Chapstick desperately and wondered why I hadn't put it on my bike in the first place. The wind, sun, and sand had done a number on my face, so when I finally got to rub the gel between my lips to soothe them, it was the best thing I'd ever felt in my life. I stuck the Chapstick in my back pocket and continued on my way.

As I sped down the hill, remembering Chip's advice again, I noticed someone being loaded into an ambulance. I prayed it wasn't any of my friends. Later, a cyclist right in front of me clipped a mile marker sign with her tire and crashed to the ground. I had to swerve to avoid hitting her and the debris flying from her bike. It happened right in front of a policeman, so I knew she had assistance, but I said a silent prayer for her and for continued safety for my friends as I tried to calm my racing heart.

Again, I passed the SBR crew, flashing them a smile as they cheered me on. They'd already spent a long day waiting around in the sun, and I could tell their energy was waning, but they still waved enthusiastically, though there were fewer of them than the previous time around.

The third time up the hill was hard, but at least I knew it was the final attack of the bike course. I used the third and final loop as an opportunity to encourage everyone I encountered, saying, "Good job, girl" or "Keep it up" to everyone I passed.

This time around, I found myself passing others more frequently than I was getting passed the last time up the mountain. The wind was still brutal and the hills relentless, but I wanted it to be finished, so I pushed on.

At one point, I needed to hear music so badly, I started singing to myself. I sang entire songs that gave me inspiration, reminding myself that when I reached the turnaround again, the hard part would be behind me. It seemed so within my reach and so far away at the same time.

I stopped at a line of Port-O-Potties to get something out of my bento box. As a volunteer helped steady me and my bike, I heard a familiar Southern drawl. I looked over to the line for the potties, and my face lit up.

"Judy!" I yelled. It was Dallas Judy, who'd predicted that I would one day find myself exactly where I was.

"Who's that?" she asked, squinting in my direction, trying to make out my features under a bike helmet and sunglasses. We'd both known we'd be on the same course, but we'd also realized we had very little chance of running into each other.

"It's Lindsey!"

"Oh my gosh, Lindsey! You're doing it! You're doing an IRONMAN! See? I told you. Never say never!"

"I'm so glad I got to see you out here. Keep going and finish strong!"

"You too!" she said, as she disappeared into the next available Port-O-Potty.

I beamed. I could think of no other person I'd rather randomly run into in the middle of a 140.6-mile race than Judy. Seeing her was exactly what I needed to help me get up the last of that hill. I jumped back on my bike and fought the gale-force winds and the worst the Arizona desert had to offer. Then the turnaround came into view for the third and final time, further confirmation I was going to make it happen.

As I flew back down the mountain, the question of timing started to nag at me again. Cyclists were pretty sparse on the course by then. I saw the dreaded sweeper going up the hill on the other side, picking off the people who weren't going to make the cutoff to start the run.

I was too tired to do the math for how fast I had to get to Transition 2, but I knew if I could just get to the run, I'd have plenty of time to finish. I pedaled my heart out to get down that hill and said a prayer that Judy would stay ahead of the sweeper as well. She'd attempted IRONMAN Arizona two years before and had to drop out. I knew she didn't want the agony of another DNF. "Come on, Judy," I said out loud, hoping my words would carry to her on the wind.

When I hit the hundred-mile mark, I had only twelve more miles to go on the bike. My neck and back ached from crouching over the aero bars for the last seven hours. Even with my padded cycling shorts, my crotch was raw from the bike seat. My swollen feet throbbed inside my cycling shoes. I ticked off those last few miles one at a time, thinking of Teri, who'd gone this same distance on the hardest course in the world while battling cancer. Without her inspiration and encouragement, I wouldn't even be competing.

I was almost there. I'd officially ridden farther than I ever had before. I was pushing new boundaries. As the crowd of spectators grew thick around me and I headed into the corral, I heard a loud "Hey!" and spotted my 6'4" brother standing taller than the rest of the people around him.

"Hey!" I yelled back. It was a typical sibling greeting. He didn't need to say anything else, and I didn't have to ability to come up with any other words.

As I dismounted and handed my bike to a volunteer, Ken was waiting off to the side. He hugged me over the orange fencing, and I nervously asked how I was doing on time.

He seemed genuinely confused because I was well ahead of the cutoff. He assured me I was fine. "You're doing awesome!" he said.

I asked another volunteer nearby if it was okay for me to take my cycling shoes off.

She said, "Sure."

I was overjoyed. The only thing that would've made me happier than taking my shoes off would've been to throw them into Tempe Town Lake, but I couldn't risk being disqualified after coming so far. Smiling, I looked back at Ken and said, "If I never put these on again, I'll be okay with that."

He yelled after me, "Go do the part you love, girl!"

I ran into T2 and found my run gear bag. I trotted into the big white tent again and changed into my running clothes: my black Asics shorts with all the pockets and my red Nike Fleet Feet racing singlet. I put on fresh socks, laced up my black and green Mizuno Riders, and shoved a couple packets of Gu into my pockets.

My running shoes had never felt as good on my feet as they did at that moment.

24: FINISHING STRONG

Depending on the strength of an athlete, finishing a triathlon with a run can be a good thing or it can be absolutely miserable. For me, it was always the best-case scenario.

As I headed through the "Run Out" arch, I felt my body relax into the comfortable familiarity of running. We were old friends, running and me, and running had always been there whenever I needed it. After a day that had begun with brutal water wrestling followed by a wind battle on a bike, running was the soft hug I needed in that moment.

I set out on the run. It was two times through the same U-shaped loop: through IRONMAN Village, down one side of Tempe Town Lake, then back the other way, across the bridge, then a long down and back along the other side of Tempe Town Lake, back over the bridge, and through the enormous crowd in the village. Then, repeat.

The crowd and the fact that I was finally running made my adrenaline soar, but I knew I had to settle into an easy pace to survive phase three of the day. I was ecstatic to be running. It wasn't fast and I knew it wouldn't be easy, but I was running. I was surprised as I passed by many athletes walking and others jogging at an even slower pace than I was.

About ten hours had passed since the cannon signaling the start of the race. I had seven hours to run a marathon. Under most circumstances, I wouldn't have worried at all. I'd completed most of my marathons in under four and a half hours. I'd also completed a challenging 50k through tough terrain on an exceedingly hot day in a little over six hours. But, once again, I faced all new territory, running a marathon after a full day of other endurance activities. I just had to keep putting one foot in front of the other.

I overheard a conversation between two girls walking as I approached them from behind. "I hate running. I'd rather do the swim twice than have to finish with the run," one girl said to the other. I shuddered at that idea, but I smiled as I ran past them, knowing I was truly in my element. It was my time to shine.

The sun was setting, casting a pinkish-purple glow on the sky, and the temperature hovered around a perfect sixty degrees. As I approached the special needs area, I didn't need anything yet, but I worried I might not have access to my bag on the second loop. I decided to pass by and continue on the course.

Not too far down the way, I came to the first aid station on the run. The smorgasbord of snacks there looked so much better than the Gu Chomps I'd pulled out of my pocket, but in my mind, I heard the advice of my friend Ray, who'd finished his first IRONMAN in Wisconsin a few weeks before: "Real food in a washing machine is never a good idea. Stick with what you know, even if everything looks good."

His point was that my churning stomach hadn't yet acclimated to the bouncing of the run and might not handle real food well. The snacks and treats laid out looked so appealing, but I knew his advice was invaluable. I munched on my chomps as I walked briskly past the tables full of options, in search of water to wash down my nourishment. When I finished, I tossed my paper cup in a trash can and picked up the pace again.

I felt a surge of energy a few minutes later as the calories and caffeine gave me a boost, but I kept my pace steady. As I neared the part of the course next to the transition area, the roar of the crowd encouraged me. I heard yelling above me and looked up on the overpass to see my family with their brightly colored signs bearing my name. Beaming, I waved up at them.

A few seconds later, I saw another familiar face in front of me. Allison, who hated the running leg of triathlon, stood there in her bright orange SBR sweatshirt, preparing to report for her volunteer duty at the finish line. She laughed and shook her head as I hollered, "I'm so happy to be running!"

I continued on, and with my name printed on my bib clipped to the race belt around my waist, I heard random strangers cheering for me, yelling "Go, Lindsey!" It was an amazing feeling to be surrounded by support from people I would likely never see again. It lifted my spirits even higher. Despite the physical pain throughout my body, I felt incredible.

As I neared the bridge to cross to the other side of the lake, I reached up to scratch an itch near my left brow. My face felt gritty, and I knew what that meant. I needed salt, soon. I knew that while on the bike I hadn't replenished enough of the sodium I'd lost. When I got to the bridge, there were some volunteers handing out some perfectly timed salt.

"Do you need sodium?" one asked as I approached.

"Yes!" I responded emphatically.

"Keep running. I'll run alongside you," he said. "Have you ever used this kind before?"

"Nope."

He proceeded to jog along next to me while giving me a little tutorial on how to use the salt tube. "Lick your thumb, flip the top open, place your wet thumb over the opening, flip it, lick the salt off your thumb, close it, and take it with you."

He handed me the tube, watched me do it once, and sent me on my way. That sodium was appropriately timed, so easy, and very necessary. I kept the tube in my left hand as I ran and periodically used it as he'd taught me.

As I came off the bridge and the course turned to the right, I recognized the place where I'd volunteered with Farrell and the rest of the group the year before. I smiled as I reminisced and accepted some water from a volunteer.

About a mile later, Ken spotted me and jumped in to run along with me for a bit. We weren't allowed to have pacers or any spectators push us on the course, but since Ken was still wearing his volunteer T-shirt, he had permission to encourage the athletes. I welcomed his company for half a mile or so since being solidly in the middle of a marathon can feel somewhat mundane.

"You're doing so great!" he said enthusiastically. I didn't know if he was being serious or not, but I believed him in that moment. He told me he'd seen my family with their Lindsey J signs and immediately recognized that my mom and my brother looked like me, so he introduced himself to them.

He gave me a high five as he turned to take a short cut to find my family to let them know how I was doing. He'd find me again later.

I continued on and moments later I noticed two braids flapping in front of me. The runner was wearing neon pink compression socks, and she was shuffling slowly, but I recognized her gait.

"Oh no, I hope that's not who I think it is," I said, just as I saw Farrell's husband, Ryan, taking a photo and her mom, Wendy, standing nearby. Farrell was a loop ahead of me and more than halfway through her second loop to my first, but I'd been hoping she was done. While I just wanted to complete this monster of a race, she had a specific time goal in mind to qualify for Kona. She looked as if she was struggling.

"Are you okay, Farrell?" I asked as I put my arm around her and squeezed.

"I don't feel good at all, Lindsey. My stomach is really upset." I frowned, and we both knew her time goal was slipping away

We walked together for a bit, and she asked how I was doing.

"I'm feeling good. I'm so happy to be doing this. This is amazing!" I said.

"I told you!" she smiled. "I'm so proud of you."

In that moment, I was completely overwhelmed with gratitude to my dear friend who'd seen something in me that I had no idea was there. She'd pushed me outside of my comfort zone, believed in me, and continued to remind me that I was capable of so much more than I realized.

While her presence there meant she wasn't likely to achieve what she wanted, it was exactly what I needed in that moment. It was another reminder that I could accomplish hard things, and that I wasn't alone in my endeavors. Farrell had seen me in some of my worst moments, and she refused to let me give up on myself. We'd both celebrated seeing me kick fear right in the face. Her words, her pride in me, reminded me how far I'd come. Here we were, two friends, out for a run, as if it were any other day. This time, it happened to be during a marathon on an IRONMAN course. We stayed together for about a mile, but then I needed to ease up a bit. That was the only time we saw each other on the course, but it was enough. We'd had our moment together.

At the next aid station, I drank some chicken broth and ate a couple of pretzels. Shortly after that, I found Ken again, who helped me up a hill on a dimly lighted part of the course. Then I went over the bridge to the other side.

I was at the halfway point of the marathon, and in the distance, I could hear the cheers of the spectators at the finish. I could hear the voice of Mike Reilly announcing the name of whoever had just crossed the finish line, but it wasn't my time to head into the chute yet. I still had another loop to go. Thirteen more miles. After 127.5 miles already, it didn't seem like a lot, but at the same time, it seemed endless.

I ran past my mom, who tried to tell me I was an IRONMAN.

"No. Not yet!" I said, "Don't jinx it!"

I ran through a crowd of strangers. I ran past some of my friends. It was all starting to blur together. Then I came to the special needs area again and slowed to a walk as I nodded yes to a volunteer who asked if I wanted my bag.

"What's your number?" he asked

"1241," I answered as I spun my race belt around to the front so he could see it.

"1241! 1241!" he shouted while volunteers searched quickly for my bag.

"Lindsey!" I heard my name and spun around to find Jess, another friend from home who was volunteering. She tackled me in a much-needed hug. I was still happy and enjoying the run, but I was tired, and I hurt.

I dug my arm warmers out of my bag and pulled them on to cover my bare skin. The temperature had dropped a few degrees when the sun went down, and my shorts and tank top were no longer enough in the mid-fifties.

I found some ibuprofen in my bag and popped it in my mouth as Jess opened a fresh bottle of water for me.

"How are you feeling?" she asked.

"I feel good," I said, which was mostly true.

I thanked her for the hug and the help, and she told me to go finish what I'd come to do. And I was off and running again.

I found myself feeling annoyed with the people in the chat groups I'd read in preparation for the event who'd said a headlamp wasn't a necessary item. The course was mostly well lit, but I could have used some extra light to assist my tired eyes, especially in the more dimly lighted parts of the course between the streetlamps.

As I ran through the crowd of IRONMAN Village on my way to the other side, I saw my group, my people. Brian jumped in and ran a few strides next to me. I noticed he was wearing a sweatshirt similar to the one I'd purchased in the IRONMAN gear tent a couple days before. The chill of the evening air had caught up to him.

He let me know they'd already loaded up the bikes and taken them back to the townhouse. After pounding my body for twelve hours, knowing I wouldn't have to deal with the additional task of retrieving my bike after finishing was a huge relief. I don't know if I let him know how much I appreciated that, but gratitude washed over me.

"How do you feel?" Brian asked as I shuffled along.

"I'm telling myself I feel okay, but I'll tell you later how I really feel," I answered. I was trying to trick myself into believing I still felt good, but the pain had really begun to set in, and I still had a long way to go.

With that, he sent me on my way to finish the race, with about a half marathon to go. I usually loved running that distance, but right then, it seemed absolutely daunting. The sounds of the village faded as I crossed the bridge and passed my previous year's volunteer aid station again. I remembered the athletes we'd cheered on at that very same spot and tried to draw strength from their inspiration.

I scanned the faces of every runner I saw, looking for someone I knew. I smiled and waved when I saw other Swim Bike Run tri club members. I spotted Barb and thought about our century ride on a beautiful day in Illinois, a building block for IRONMAN.

At one point, I walked for a while with some random guys. I needed the camaraderie and the distraction of new conversation. I don't remember what we talked about, but it was a nice break from my internal monologue of "Just keep going, keep putting one foot in front of the other" repeating in my brain. I was trying to get to the next aid station, and then the next one. I couldn't think any further than that.

I slowed to a walk, put my hand on my hip, and was surprised how badly it hurt. Even the slightest graze of my fingertips against my core felt as if I were resting a cinderblock on my waist. There wasn't a single part of me that wasn't feeling the pain of every step.

When I arrived at the darkest part of the run, due to a burned-out streetlight at the base of the only real hill on the run course, Ken was waiting for me. He turned on his iPhone and used it as a flashlight to illuminate the path in front of me. He helped me get up the hill, reminding me of the time I'd been lost in the woods as we ran the Smoky Mountain Relay. He'd gone into the woods to find me, taken me by the hand, and pulled my exhausted, broken body up that hill to the next exchange. Then he reminded me that the following year, in that same leg of that same race, I hadn't gotten lost and hadn't needed help. He'd still been there anyway to run me out of those woods, just because.

Before I knew it, we were at the top of the hill, and Ken sent me on to the next aid station.

"You've only got a 5k to go, and you've got plenty of time. You are going to do this!" he encouraged me. "See you at the finish!"

Only a 5k. My 5k personal record was seven minutes per mile. I wasn't running anywhere near that pace. Prior to race day, I'd estimated a time goal of fourteen hours. It was already beyond the fourteen-hour mark, but I still had a shot at finishing in under fifteen. Not that it really mattered. The only real goal was finishing before the cutoff. Even if I walked to the finish line, I would still make it.

I didn't want to walk any more than I absolutely had to. I tried to run, but it hurt, so I walked. That hurt too, both physically and emotionally, as it kept me from the finish. My brain hurt from trying to convince my body to keep going.

With just over a mile to go, nearly every athlete on the course with me was walking. Several of them were wrapped in mylar blankets, shivering and trying to make it to the finish any way they could.

At that point, I made a decision: no more walking. It didn't matter how slowly I jogged. I thought of Teri and her term *slogging* for slow jogging. I didn't want to walk the last mile, only to run when I saw the finish line, so I slogged along, but I smiled.

As I got closer to the finish, my smile got bigger. Everyone who saw me said, "Wow, look at that smile! Are you still having fun?"

I laughed, I smiled, I ran. I was running the last mile of an IRONMAN. I thought of all the miles behind me—all of the long, painful, grueling miles. I thought of how much I'd accomplished to get to that moment. I thought of the people waiting in anticipation for me to come into the finishers' chute, including my own daughter. I was teaching her an invaluable lesson about breaking down barriers to reach her dreams and about never giving up.

I could hear Mike Reilly again, and I didn't have far to go until he'd call my name. More spectators lined the course, and the crowd was getting louder.

I turned, and I could see the finishers' chute about a block away. My mom's friend Elaine, who had volunteered earlier in the day, called out to me and gave me a high five. I could feel myself beaming as if it were lifting me off the ground and carrying me into that chute.

All feeling of pain disappeared, replaced by the roar of the crowd, the elation of seeing the finish line in front of me, and the relief that I could soon stop. I left every time I'd ever let anyone make me feel small behind me on that course. Over those 140.6 miles, I'd picked up the missing pieces of my soul and put them back into place where they belonged. I loomed larger than life.

I'd learned the most valuable lessons of my life that day: No matter what happens, keep going. Learn to embrace the suck. And whatever you do, keep smiling all the way to the finish.

To my right, I saw the same neon sign with my name on it that I'd seen fifteen hours before, and my family right behind it. I high fived them and smacked my sign. It was a "Hell, yeah!" moment, knowing without a doubt I'd crushed what I'd gone out there to do. I could see the time clock, and it read fifteen hours and one minute. Allison smiled and waited to catch me on the other side.

With just steps to go, I pressed the fingertips of my right hand to my lips, and as I passed under the finish line, I raised them toward the sky, blowing a kiss to heaven, as Mike Reilly announced, "Lindsey Jacobs, you *are* an IRONMAN finisher!"

RAMBLING RUNNER GIRL'S
TIMELINE OF SIGNIFICANT RACES

October 7, 2001: Chicago Marathon

October 12, 2008: Chicago Marathon

October 19, 2009: Detroit Marathon

October 10, 2010: Chicago Marathon

November 14, 2010: Malibu Marathon

August 2011: Quebec City Marathon (Canceled)

December 4, 2011: Dallas Whiterock Marathon

August 25, 2012: Lake Saint Louis Olympic Distance Triathlon

October 7, 2012: Chicago Marathon

May 5, 2013: Vancouver Marathon

July 21, 2013: Racine IRONMAN® 70.3® Triathlon

August 24, 2013: Lake Saint Louis Olympic Distance Triathlon

October 13, 2013: Chicago Marathon

November 10, 2013: Skippo 30k

July 12, 2014: Psycho Wyco 50k

August 23, 2014: Lake Saint Louis Olympic Distance Triathlon

October 4, 2014: Border Wars Half Distance Triathlon

November 16, 2014: IRONMAN Arizona 140.6

ACKNOWLEDGMENTS

To my Lord and Savior, Jesus Christ: None of this would have been possible without all that You've done for me. All those nights I cried out to You, "Jesus, be enough," You always showed up; You were always enough. And so much more.

My social runners, Fleet Feet coworkers, Swim Bike Run peeps, Smokin' Aces, and Hot Mess Crew: There are too many of you to name individually. Whether you were mentioned by name or not in these pages, you all played a huge part in this journey. For all the miles you put in with me, I can't thank you enough. Thank you for being there and keeping things fun, even when they were hard. I love you all!

Judy: From the day we randomly met on a charter bus in Dallas, you predicted all of it! Thank you for opening your hotel room to a stranger and your heart to a new friend. Thank you for being an incredible part of my story and a cheerleader to so many.

Lindsey Farrell: Thank you for immediately recognizing the strength and light inside me. You reminded me that it was there again and again and again. Thank you for not letting me forget. I believe it now.

Steve Carrell: Thank you for being my training partner. You held my hand, dragged me along when I didn't want to keep going, and kept pushing me. Whether you were laughing with me or at me, you always kept me laughing. Also, thank you for going to the movies with me when no one else would.

Britta: Thank you for always believing in me, especially in my worst moments, when I didn't believe in myself. Even when there were hundreds of miles between us, emotionally, you never left my side. You never doubted I'd make a comeback. I don't know how to ever repay that. Love you.

Teri: You are *the* reason I dug deep within myself and kept going no matter how hard it got. Thank you for your unmatchable inspiration and for the beautiful gift of your friendship.

Mom: I don't even know what to say. "Thank you" doesn't seem close to enough when I consider how much you've done. You never stopped loving me, supporting me, and believing in me. For all the times you told me I'd write a book someday, this is for you.

Dad: When you left, you took a part of my soul with you, and I lost my way for a while. I'm sorry it took me so long to realize that, in its place, you left a piece of yourself with me. Thank you for all the lessons you taught me in preparation for your early departure. Thank you for all the miles you ran with me, all the encouragement, and your unconditional love and support. I miss you every single day, but I'm so thankful for the hope I have to run with you again someday. My teacher, my coach, my father, my friend. "It is well, it is well with my soul."

Ally: My baby girl, having you at the finish line of my IRONMAN was a dream come true, second only to being a mom to you and your brothers. I hope that in my humanness, I've taught you that it's okay to make mistakes, as long as you own them; to be unapologetically exactly who you are no matter what anyone else tells you; and to go after your dreams with every ounce of life and passion in your being. Don't let anyone make you feel small, not ever. And if anyone ever tries, remind them who you are. I say it all the time: God knew exactly what He was doing when He gave you to me. Love, Mama Bear.

My boys, Ethan and Silas, and my bonus boy, Greyson: You guys couldn't be more different, and I wouldn't have it any other way. I love the uniqueness you possess, and my biggest wish for each of you is that you find your passion and pursue it with everything you've got. Be true to who you are, laugh a lot, love with your whole heart, live every minute with reckless abandon, and apologize when you need to. Thank you for always keeping me on my toes, for giving me a reason to laugh every day, and for the light and kindness you all bring to this world. I love you guys.

Brian: Neither of our lives was easy, but everything that happened to both of us brought us to each other. There's no one else I want as my adventure partner. Thank you for always going along with my crazy ideas and for supporting me through them. You accept me as I am, and for that I'm abundantly grateful. I'm still smitten. Scarf.

BOOK CLUB DISCUSSION QUESTIONS

There were times when Lindsey felt trapped. Discuss a time that you felt trapped. How did you feel? How did you overcome your fears? What did you do to get untrapped? Is being trapped an illusion or is it real?

Does anything in your life make you feel like you're drowning? What is it? How do you continue to breathe?

Swimming can be considered a metaphor for life situations. How do you relate to that?

Is there anything that you can coast through in life? What is it? How do you tackle it in a way that still allows you to put forth your full effort? Is it okay to coast? Why or why not?

What are your biggest fears? How do you face them? What were Lindsey's fears, and how did she overcome them?

What's been the biggest challenge in your life? How did you get through it? Relate that challenge to a triathlon.

Who's been there to encourage you in your darkest moments? Who's been there to cheer you on when you needed it most? Who's been there to help you celebrate your accomplishments? On the flip side, who has deterred you from becoming all you can be? How do you handle those relationships?

What are your biggest weaknesses? What are your strengths? Are they the same? Why or why not?

What have been your biggest losses? How did you deal with them? Were you able to turn them into positive experiences? If so, how?

When you make a mistake, how do you move forward? How did Lindsey move forward after setbacks?

What brings you the greatest joy? How can you bring more of that into your life?

ABOUT THE AUTHOR

Lindsey Jacobs lives in Saint Louis, Missouri, with her husband, kids, and their pug, Rizzo. She graduated from nursing school in 2017 and now enjoys working as an OB/GYN nurse. In her spare time, she loves to explore, run, write, and read. Lindsey hasn't made it to the Boston Marathon yet, but she's determined to chase that dream until she's fulfilled it. This is her first book.

CPSIA information can be obtained
at www.ICGtesting.com
Printed in the USA
LVHW080745130220
646779LV00002B/9